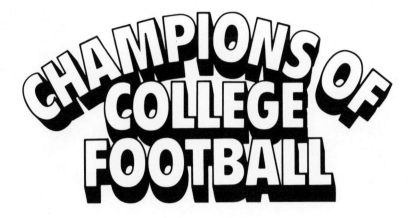

Bill Libby

HAWTHORN BOOKS, INC.
PUBLISHERS/*New York*

This book is for Indiana University.
Its football team may not have won
national titles, but its journalism department
gave me a marvelous education.

Contents

Acknowledgments

The author wishes to thank for their help John McKay and all of the coaches, players and publicists of all of the colleges who cooperated in the task. He wishes to thank especially Forest Foster of the Tournament of Roses, Gil Sloan of the Orange Bowl, Joseph Katz of the New Orleans Mid-Winter Sports Association, Bill Morgan of the Southwest Conference, Jim Perry of USC, Vic Kelley of UCLA, Charles Thornton of Alabama, Tab Bennett of Illinois, Mark Lookabaugh of Washington, Ben Mintz of Cornell, Bob Kinney and Kenneth Rapp of Army, E. S. Fabricius of Penn, Dan Magill of Georgia, Will Perry of Michigan, Nick Vista of Michigan State, Dave Matthews and Jean Zwicky of Stanford, Jones Ramsey of Texas, Haywood Harris of Tennessee, Otis Dypwick of Minnesota, Mike Krauss of Chicago, Phil Langan of Princeton, Don Bryant of Nebraska, John Morris of Penn State and Peter Easton of Yale.

The author wishes also to thank Ben Olan of the Associated Press, Jim Cour of United Press International, Rich Roberts of the Long Beach *Independent Press Telegram* and Buddy Dyer of the Helms Citizens Savings Hall of Fame, as well as all the writers and historians whose words and statistics contributed immeasurably to this volume. He wishes to thank Johnny Johnson and Wen Roberts of Photography, Inc., of Inglewood, California, and all of the photographers whose work appears on these pages. And, finally, he wishes to thank his editors, Charles Heckelmann and Carolyn Trager, without whom there would not be this book and it would not be what it is.

9

College Football's National Champions

(An arbitrary list)

Year	Team	Coach	Outstanding Players
1900	Yale (12–0–0)	Malcolm McBride	Skim Brown, Bill Fincke
1901	Michigan (11–0–0)	Fielding Yost	Willie Heston, Tug Wilson
1902	Michigan (11–0–0)	Fielding Yost	Willie Heston, Tug Wilson
1903	Princeton (11–0–0)	Doc Hillebrand	John DeWitt, Dana Kafer
1904	Minnesota (13–0–0)	Harry Williams	
1905	Chicago (9–0–0)	Amos A. Stagg	Walter Eckersall, Mark Catlin
1906	Princeton (9–0–1)	Bill Roper	Jim Cooney, Casper Wister
1907	Yale (9–0–1)	Samuel Morse	Tad Jones, Clarence Alcott
1908	Penn (11–0–1)	Sol Metzger	Bill Hollenback
1909	Yale (10–0–0)	Howard Jones	Ted Coy, John Kilpatrick
1910	Washington (6–0–0)	Gil Dobie	Bill Coyle, Walt Wand
1911	Carlisle (11–1–0)	Pop Warner	Jim Thorpe, Joe Guyon
1912	Harvard (9–0–0)	Percy Haughton	Charley Brickley, Sam Felton
1913	Notre Dame (7–0–0)	G. W. Philbrook	Gus Dorais, Knute Rockne
1914	Illinois (7–0–0)	Bob Zuppke	Bert Macomber
1915	Pitt (8–0–0)	Pop Warner	Bob Peck, Jim DeHart
1916	Army (9–0–0)	Charley Daly	Elmer Oliphant

11

Year	Team	Coach	Outstanding Players
1917	Georgia Tech (9–0–0)	John Heisman	Joe Guyon, Ev Strupper
1918	Pitt (4–0–0)	Pop Warner	George McLaren, Bob Peck
1919	Notre Dame (9–0–0)	Knute Rockne	George Gipp
1920	California (9–0–0)	Andy Smith	Brick Muller
1921	Iowa (7–0–0)	Howard Jones	Duke Slater, Aubrey Devine
1922	Cornell (8–0–0)	Gil Dobie	Eddie Kaw, George Pfann
1923	Illinois (8–0–0)	Bob Zuppke	Red Grange
1924	Notre Dame (10–0–0)	Knute Rockne	"The Four Horsemen"
1925	Alabama (10–0–0)	Wallace Wade	Johnny Mack Brown
1926	Navy (9–0–1)	Bill Ingram	Frank Wickhorst, Tom Hamilton
1927	Texas A&M (8–0–1)	Dana X. Bible	Joel Hunt
1928	Georgia Tech (10–0–0)	Bill Alexander	Pete Pund
1929	Tulane (9–0–0)	Bernie Bierman	Billy Banker, Jerry Dalrymple
1930	Notre Dame (10–0–0)	Knute Rockne	Frank Carideo, Joe Savoldi
1931	Tennessee (9–0–1)	Bob Neyland	Herman Hickman, Beattie Feathers
1932	USC (10–0–0)	Howard Jones	Ernie Smith, Orv Mohler
1933	Princeton (9–0–0)	Fritz Crisler	John Weller
1934	Alabama (10–0–0)	Frank Thomas	Don Hutson, Dixie Howell
1935	Minnesota (8–0–0)	Bernie Bierman	Ed Widseth, Andy Uram
1936	Northwestern (7–1–0)	Lynn Waldorf	Steve Toth
1937	Pitt (9–0–1)	Jock Sutherland	Marshall Goldberg, Tony Matisi
1938	Tennessee (11–0–0)	Bob Neyland	Bob Suffridge, Bowden Wyatt
1939	Texas A&M (11–0–0)	Homer Norton	John Kimbrough, Marsh Robnett
1940	Stanford (10–0–0)	Clark Shaughnessy	Frankie Albert, Norm Standlee
1941	Minnesota (8–0–0)	Bernie Bierman	Bruce Smith, Dick Wildung
1942	Georgia (9–1–0)	Wally Butts	Frank Sinkwich, Charlie Trippi

Year	Team	Coach	Outstanding Players
1943	Notre Dame (9–1–0)	Frank Leahy	Angelo Bertelli, Jim White
1944	Army (9–0–0)	Red Blaik	Glenn Davis, Doc Blanchard
1945	Army (9–0–0)	Red Blaik	Glenn Davis, Doc Blanchard, Tex Coulter
1946	Notre Dame (8–0–1)	Frank Leahy	John Lujack, George Connor
1947	Michigan (10–0–0)	Fritz Crisler	Bob Chappius, Bump Elliott
1948	Michigan (9–0–0)	B. Oosterban	Al Wistert, Pete Elliott
1949	Notre Dame (10–0–0)	Frank Leahy	Leon Hart, Emil Sitko
1950	Kentucky (11–1–0)	Bear Bryant	Babe Parilli, Bob Gain
1951	Maryland (10–0–0)	Jim Tatum	Bob Ward, Jack Scarbath
1952	Michigan State (9–0–0)	Biggie Munn	Don McAuliffe, Billy Wells
1953	Notre Dame (9–0–1)	Frank Leahy	John Lattner, Art Hunter
1954	UCLA (9–0–0)	Red Sanders	Bob Davenport, Jack Ellena
1955	Oklahoma (11–0–0)	Bud Wilkinson	Tom McDonald, Jerry Tubbs
1956	Oklahoma (10–0–0)	Bud Wilkinson	Tom McDonald, Jerry Tubbs, Clen Thomas
1957	Auburn (10–0–0)	Shug Jordan	Jim Phillips, Zeke Smith
1958	LSU (11–0–0)	Paul Dietzel	Billy Cannon, Warren Rabb
1959	Syracuse (11–0–0)	B. Schwartzwalder	Ernie Davis, Roger Davis
1960	Mississippi (10–0–1)	John Vaught	Jake Gibbs, Jim Dunaway
1961	Alabama (11–0–0)	Bear Bryant	LeeRoy Joran, Bill Neighbors
1962	USC (11–0–0)	John McKay	Hal Bedsole, Pete Beathard
1963	Texas (11–0–0)	Darrel Royal	Tommy Nobis, Scott Appleton
1964	Arkansas (11–0–0)	Frank Broyles	Bobby Burnett
1965	Michigan State (10–1–0)	Duffy Daugherty	Bubba Smith, George Webster
1966	Notre Dame (9–0–1)	Ara Parseghian	Nick Eddy, Jim Lynch
1967	USC (10–1–0)	John McKay	O. J. Simpson, Ron Yary

13

Year	Team	Coach	Outstanding Players
1968	Ohio State (10–0–0)	Woody Hayes	Dave Foley, Jim Otis
1969	Texas (11–0–0)	Darrel Royal	Bob McKay, Jim Bertelsen
1970	Nebraska (11–0–1)	Bob Devaney	Bob Newton, John Rodgers
1971	Nebraska (13–0–0)	Bob Devaney	John Rodgers, Willie Harper
1972	USC (12–0–0)	John McKay	Anthony Davis, Charles Young
1973	Notre Dame (11–0–0)	Ara Parseghian	Dave Casper, Mike Townsend
1974	Oklahoma (11–0–0)	Barry Switzer	Joe Washington, Rod Shoate

1

The Kings Are Crowned

ON THE FINAL night of 1973 that year's champion of college football was crowned. The teams of two great universities, Notre Dame and Alabama, met to settle the title on New Year's Eve in the Sugar Bowl classic in New Orleans.

Both teams were undefeated and untied, with great coaches, Ara Parseghian and Paul "Bear" Bryant, whose records ranked among the best in the history of this sport. It is not often that 1 game at season's end settles this annual award, but almost all agreed this one would.

An estimated 40 million persons watched on television across the country. More than 85,000 persons packed into ancient Tulane Stadium to see the contest. The press box bulged with reporters prepared to put the story's outcome in print for posterity.

There are more important things in life, but for a few hours it would not seem so. The buildup had been beyond belief and put a pressure on the participants that threatened to tear them apart. These were young men who had an ability to play this game better than most, and while most of them would go on to do other things, they had reached early what might be the most memorable moment of their lives.

The drums rolled and the bands blared away, filling the arena with color and sound. Gaudy floats circled the playing area. Healthy and attractive young cheerleaders, their faces shining with excitement, leaped on long legs into the air, shaking their fists at the fans in a demand for demonstrations of enthusiasm for their teams. The noise rose in the night.

The players poured out of tunnels onto the green field, illuminated by towering rows of blazing arc lights, and the fans stood and hollered for them. The helmeted players wore their heavily padded uniforms—"The Fighting Irish" of Notre Dame in their blue and gold, "The Crimson Tide" of Alabama in their crimson and white. They seemed enormous. Many were.

There were a hundred of them, regulars and subs, and they circled together in an explosion of enthusiasm, encouraging one another in their determination to win. They were dedicated. They had practiced to the point of exhaustion. They had played and won hard games. Now they had reached the game that meant the national title.

The dreams of many had died along the way. Few ever got this far. These had. This was their year. One team would win and one would lose. If they tied, the title would go to another team. A tie would be like losing. They thought only of winning. But only one would win.

Their circles separated and the starters streamed onto the field. The tension thickened as the rivals faced one another under a glaring spotlight.

The kickoff! The ball was place-kicked through the cool, damp night air, a receiver caught it and began to move with it behind blockers as defenders drove at him. Tacklers were blocked, the runner was tackled and the ball game had begun.

It seemed impossible for any game to live up to the buildup of this one, but this one did. It was a bitter battle from beginning to end.

It was, of course, imperfect. The players were paled by the

pressure and hurt by the heavy hitting. There were 9 fumbles and dropped passes and intercepted passes and missed place-kicks and almost 100 yards in penalties from 8 rule infractions.

But there also were accurate passes, clever catches, spectacular runs, brutal blocks, violent tackles—a great deal of superb play from start to finish by two college teams as skilled as any that have played football. Before the drama was done, the thrills would come fast and furious and the excitement would be almost more than a sports fan could stand.

The lead changed hands 7 times.

Notre Dame drove 64 yards for the only score of the first quarter. Wayne Bullock, a 220-pound fullback from Newport News, Virginia, bulled over from 1 yard out to make it 6-0. But Bob Thomas missed the extra point, kicking so hard the ball hooked wide. He hung his head in dejection, unaware what fate held in store for him.

In the second session, Alabama moved 48 yards to tie the score. Randy Billingsley knifed over from the 5 to even the count. Bill Davis place-kicked perfectly to put the Crimson Tide on top, 7-6.

On the ensuing kickoff, Al Hunter, a bespectacled freshman from Greenville, North Carolina, broke free behind blocks and sprinted 93 yards to shove the Fighting Irish in front again. By then the fans were in a frenzy.

Quarterback Tom Clements from McKees Rocks, Pennsylvania, an agile player and accurate passer, threw to Pete Demmerle of New Canaan, Connecticut, for the 2-point conversion that made up for the missed kick and built the edge to 14-7.

Before the first half ended, Davis reduced the Notre Dame advantage to 14-10 with a 39-yard field goal. The issue was far from settled as the two teams wearily regrouped at intermission while the marching bands and floats briefly filled the field.

Thirty minutes of playing time remained and Alabama emerged from its dressing room seemingly strengthened by Bear Bryant's words of wisdom. At the start of the second half, his players seemed inspired.

Relentlessly they drove 93 yards in 11 plays. Wilbur Jackson, a jarring runner, ripped in from the 5 for a touchdown. Davis place-kicked the Tide to a 17–14 lead and rebel banners waved wildly.

Aroused, Alabama's defensive unit smothered Notre Dame's tattempt to retaliate. The Irish had to punt the ball back to the Crimson Tide.

However, here a fumble proved pivotal. Notre Dame took over on the 12. Eric Penick of Cleveland, Ohio, sprinted into the zone on the first play following the critical turnover and the Irish had vaulted back on top. Thomas made his kick and it was 21–17 after 3 periods.

Exhaustion, both emotional and physical, worked on the sweat-soaked, dirt-smeared players. Time to turn the tide was growing short now. The powerful players in the trenches up front bruised away at one another as the contest spun toward its conclusion.

Behind the blocking of such as 240-pound Buddy Brown, the southerners mounted a march. It seemed to stall at the Notre Dame 25-yard line. With third down and 7 yards to go, Alabama was in trouble. But the Bear sent in a trick play. It was one Notre Dame had used itself but did not expect here.

A reserve Alabama quarterback, Richard Todd, took the ball from center and handed off to running back Mike Stock. As Stock swung wide as if to run and the Notre Dame defenders moved up to meet him, Todd drifted downfield.

Stock suddenly stopped and threw the ball. Todd, all alone, caught it and scored with it.

The sudden strike shot Alabama back into the lead, 23–21, and set off what seemed almost a victory celebration on the part of its fans. But then Davis muffed the place-kick and Notre Dame remained within reach. At the kickoff, its supporters pleaded with the Irish players to pull off a miracle of some sort. Little time was left now.

Commented Clements later, "We knew what we had to do. We had the ability to move to a score. All we had to do was to get within range of a field goal. All we had to do was to maintain our poise. All we had to do was resist the pressure and use our ability."

Parseghian, suffering on the sidelines with the rest of his team, pacing up and down nervously, screaming instructions at his offensive unit, later admitted, "There is not much a coach can do at such a time. You've prepared your players for just such times. You only hope you've prepared them properly."

Bryant said, "We had the ball game then, and we knew it, but we also knew we could let it get away from us. Well, it was time to see who was the best team. We thought we were the best, but we knew they were good, too. There's not much to choose between two such teams, you know."

Sometimes no more than a point. Or two. Alabama had 2 points on its foe with the second hand sweeping around the clock and the minutes ticking off and time running out.

Notre Dame took control of the ball on its 20-yard line and began to move it. Desperately, but steadily, it drove the ball downfield. Three times Clements was trapped trying to pass and three times he eluded the defenders, squirmed free and ran for gains to keep the march moving.

On third down, with 1 yard to go at the Alabama 45, Clements faked a keeper-run and threw daringly downfield to Dave Casper. A 250-pound all-American tight end, Casper was covered by 2 Tide defenders and seemed smothered, but the big guy muscled his way beyond the backs, reached up with his two big hands and pulled the ball in for a 30-yard gain that kept the Irish going.

'Bama bore down. The Tide thwarted the Irish at the goal line. On fourth down, Parseghian sent in Thomas to try for a field goal that would kick the Irish into the lead.

The senior specialist from Rochester, New York, was well aware of his earlier miss. "I was trying too hard and kicked too hard. The ball curved and I could have killed myself. Now it was all up to me," he recalled later.

He didn't kick too hard this time. He kicked just right. In a sudden hush of emotion, the ball was snapped to the holder and set down and the youngster drilled it between the uprights as the great arena exploded in sound. Suddenly, Notre Dame had regained the lead, 24–23.

There was a little time left. Those on the Alabama side screamed for one final comeback. The Crimson players tried and failed, frustrated by the Notre Dame defense. Rather than gamble on fourth down with long yardage to go, Bryant called for a punt he hoped would pin Notre Dame deep in its territory.

A 69-yard punt put Notre Dame in the shadow of its goal line. Just as Alabama dreams were dying, its hopes rose anew. The Crimson smeared an Irish run. And another. One more and Notre Dame would have to punt from its own end zone, a situation that would give Alabama one last chance to win.

Now there was something Parseghian could do. Cursed for being too cautious in settling for a 10–10 tie with Michigan State in a memorable game that had preserved Notre Dame's last national championship 8 seasons earlier, the coach called for a daring play in an attempt to retain possession of the ball.

On third down and 8 yards to go on the 2-yard line, Clements faked a handoff to a runner as Alabama defenders charged toward the rush, faded back into his end zone and lofted a long pass toward the sidelines by the Bama bench.

Uncovered on the unexpected play, Robin Weber, a towering, powerful youngster from Dallas, Texas, reached up and caught the ball as he crashed out of bounds into the men in the crimson jerseys.

He came out holding the ball aloft. The 35-yard play kept the ball for the Irish and preserved their precarious position on the throne.

A few plays later, Clements collapsed happily to the ground with the precious pigskin cradled in his arms, the final gun sounded and Notre Dame was the national champion—by the slender margin of a single point.

While the famed "Victory March" was played loudly, Irish fans stood and cheered, and a couple of them in that vast stadium held aloft a banner that read, "God Made Notre Dame No. 1." The Irish players swept their coach up on their shoulders and paraded triumphantly across the field with him. Humbled, the losing coach walked across the battlefield to shake the winner's hand.

Alabama fans stood and stared in silence at the scene, deeply depressed as their dejected players, heads down, walked away past a pretty cheerleader who wept with her sorrow. The players went into their dressing room and sat down, suddenly spent with the weariness of wasted efforts and dashed dreams, while in the other team's quarters a wild victory celebration erupted.

To the victor go the laurels, and to Notre Dame went the votes and the trophies that established it as the champion of college football for that year. "It is something the top teams always go for, but which few get and no one ever really expects. It is what we in college football work for and dream of. And when you get it, no one can ever take it away from you," the winning coach said.

Which is true, but only to a point. It is that team's title for that year and is indelibly inscribed in the record books as such. It is history and permanent. And yet it is also true that it is only out on loan, a season at a time, and a new championship will be won one year later. And seldom can one club claim the crown beyond dispute.

Any time a Notre Dame team captures college football's championship it is especially significant because the Fighting Irish have had the most impressive history in the sport. They have won or shared 19 national titles, compared to 11 for Michigan, 10 for Alabama and lesser numbers for others over the last 75 years. However, few were unanimous.

Arbitrarily, in this book, we credit them with 11 crowns, Michigan and Southern Cal with 4 each, 7 teams with 3 each, 6 teams with 2 each and another 22 teams with 1 each. Arbitrarily we credit 40 teams with national titles over the years, but more than 60 teams can claim at least a share of the laurels one season or another without being unreasonable.

The night after Notre Dame nosed out Alabama to gain general recognition as the 1973 champion, a powerful Penn State team scored a triumph in the Orange Bowl to complete a 12-game season undefeated and untied, which entitled it to claim a share of the throne even if its supporters were outnumbered by those of the Irish. Penn State did not get the top trophies because its schedule was considered less demanding than Notre Dame's, but the Nittany Lions overcame every challenge they encountered, too, and must go down in the record books—and in this book—as one of the great teams of all time.

It is the author's purpose in this book to single out the great teams of all time in college football. The book begins in 1900 because it was at the turn of the century that this sport really started to assume its shape as we know it today. Thus we are considering a round 75 years of this sport's history.

It is unfortunate that there is not a title tournament to crown a champion each year. Any one of several systems would suffice. But there is not.

In the early years, one or two men took it upon themselves to declare champions of college football annually, and these declarations generally have been accepted although they really lacked authority.

In 1936 the Associated Press started to poll sportswriters to determine yearly rankings and season's-end kings, and in 1950 United Press International began to put the vote to a panel of coaches, but there often have been deep divisions of opinion between the two.

Over the years, other groups such as the Football Writers' Association of America, the National Football Foundation and the Helms Hall of Fame have crowned clubs, but these also did not often agree with each other. For many years the season's-end bowl games were not included in the consideration, although these annual classic contests usually matched most of the top teams and thus provided an important measurement of quality that should not have been ignored.

In this book we use all the yardsticks available to us. Where the vote was sufficiently heavy in favor of one team or another we usually accepted this no matter how unreasonable the decision may now seem. However, where there could be no clear-cut champion, we—with the benefit of hindsight, the long-range view, bowl results and other measurements— arbitrarily selected one, as listed in the front of this volume. And we have arbitrarily ranked the top teams of the early years.

At the same time in the back of the book we also have included the rankings and champions that have been produced by the major groups over the years, along with year-by-year listings of the clubs that logically could claim shares of the championships.

The latter list may be the most meaningful. It is not a ranking. It includes those teams whose records entitled them to claim the crown in a given year. But the second-best team one year may have been eliminated from that year's list because of a loss to the best team.

We also have broken down three-quarters of a century to total up the teams and coaches who have won or shared the most titles, and it is these that dominate this volume. All of the greats of 75 years of college football get credit herein.

Some surprises surface. It is well known that "The Big Three" of Yale, Harvard and Princeton dominated the early days of college football. But maybe many did not realize that many other teams merited shares of the championships in those years.

Even in the first decade, Michigan, Minnesota, Wisconsin and Nebraska produced powerhouses in the Midwest. Notre Dame was a championship contender as early as 1903, 10 years before Gus Dorais's passes to Knute Rockne transformed football.

Southern schools such as Vanderbilt, Auburn and LSU were early powers. So was Washington in the Far West and a little later, Texas, Texas A&M and Oklahoma in the Southwest. And early on, Penn, Army, Pitt and Cornell threatened the East's glamor guys.

There have been sharp shifts in power over the years, and in perusing these pages it is well to remember that there were eras in which Chicago, Marquette, Lafayette, Washington & Jefferson, Fordham, Carnegie Tech, Santa Clara, St. Mary's and many more teams that no longer play top-level college football were of championship caliber.

Indeed, while it has been a long time since Ivy League teams bid for national laurels, one may be surprised to discover that some of them ranked with the country's best clubs as late as the World War II period.

Today, Notre Dame, Ohio State, Michigan, Alabama, Oklahoma, Nebraska, Southern Cal, Penn State and Texas seem to be the most dominant, but many other schools have produced powerhouses and champions in other days.

The great teams of all time are recognized here, season by season, as well as many of the great games of all time, spectacular contests that settled national titles. These include memorable moments such as Roy Riegels's celebrated wrong-way run. Did you know it determined the champion of that year?

The great teams had great stars, from Willie Heston, Walt Eckersall and Tad Jones to Don Hutson, Glenn Davis and Doc Blanchard; from Jim Thorpe, Charley Brickley and Brick Muller to Angelo Bertelli, Johnny Lujack, and Leon Hart; from Red Grange, George Gipp and "The Four Horsemen" to Tommy Nobis, O. J. Simpson and Johnny Rodgers. All are prominent in these pages.

And, of course, the great teams had great coaches, from Hurry Up Yost, Amos Alonzo Stagg, Gloomy Gil Dobie, Pop Warner, Howard Jones, Bernie Bierman, Bob Neyland and

Knute Rockne to Frank Leahy, Bud Wilkinson, Bear Bryant, Darrell Royal, Woody Hayes, Bob Devaney, John McKay and Ara Parseghian. Football is a coach's game more than any other, and these and other immortals are featured in what follows.

The prize captured by Notre Dame on that recent New Year's Eve in New Orleans may be as much mythical as real, but it is sought by and has been chased by college clubs for close to a century now. Players recruited from towns across the country put on a university's uniform, as did those who donned the golden helmets of the Fighting Irish and are forever after identified with that school, its city and its state.

A lad from Rochester, New York, put a place-kick through the crossbars and became a part of the incredible legend of football in South Bend, Indiana, just as others from other places have helped put other schools on top in other years. A single point parted winner from loser, champion from also-ran. It is a cruel contest, this annual chase for the national title, but one of endless excitement and eternal interest.

Some day perhaps, as some wish, a panel will pick the best two or four teams of the season following the bowl games and there will be a playoff clearly crowning a champion. Until that day, arguments will rage annually. Reading about them, the reader can make his or her own selections. Here are the arguments. Here are the champions of college football.

2

The Early Days

FOOTBALL IS BELIEVED to have been born in ancient Greece, but that infant bore little resemblance to the sport that has grown up to become this country's big game. Then as many as a hundred men on a side pushed and shoved over an open field to move an inflated ball across an end line.

As it spread around the world and entered England, it split into two games—a sort of soccer, in which the ball was kicked, not handled, and running was prohibited; and a sort of rugby, in which you could run with the ball as well as kick it and play was continuous.

Our game grew out of rugby as the number of players to a team was reduced and playing fields were reduced to more reasonable proportions. In the middle 1800s, Harvard students split into sides for an annual football game on what came to be called Bloody Monday. It was so rough it was barred in 1860.

However, in 1865, rival New Jersey schools, the College of New Jersey, which became Princeton, and Rutgers disputed rights to a Revolutionary War cannon, which can be considered football's first trophy. They settled on a sporting event to determine possession, and Princeton routed its rival in the "New York Game," which became baseball, by the awesome score of 40-2.

Seeking revenge, Rutgers issued a challenge to its foe to a rematch in a game of football. The challenge was accepted and the contest was played on the afternoon of the sixth of November. It has come to be called intercollegiate football's first game. Some 25 students on each side stripped to their shirt-sleeves and had at it. Wearing scarlet caps to distinguish themselves, Rutgers prevailed, 6 goals to 4. In a rematch at Princeton, the hosts prevailed, 8 goals to none.

In November of 1870, students from Columbia played at Princeton and were defeated 6 goals to 3. That year Princeton also trimmed Rutgers, 8 goals to none. In 1872, Yale hosted Columbia at New Haven and won by 3 goals to none. Gradually the game spread from school to school, and more regular meetings were arranged.

Rutgers, Princeton, Columbia and Yale held the first formal football meeting in 1873 and created the first formal rules. The field was set at 140 yards in length and 70 yards in width. The games were to be played in two 45-minute halves. The only way to score was to kick or bat the ball across the opposing goal line. No running was permitted.

Harvard students had started to play the game seriously in 1872, but since they preferred to permit running with the ball, they went their own way. Meanwhile, students at McGill University in Montreal had devised a variation of the new game in which a touchdown could be scored by running the ball across the goal line.

Harvard invited McGill to Cambridge for a series of games in May of 1874. Under Harvard rules, the hosts won, 3 goals to none. Under McGill rules, the game was scoreless. However, Harvard liked and adopted McGill rules for a third game, which the Crimson captured, 3 touchdowns to none.

Harvard then challenged Yale. A compromise was reached in the rules, but they favored Harvard, which won in

November of 1875 in New Haven before 2,000 excited spectators, 4 goals to none.

One of the spectators was Walter Camp, a 16-year-old high school student. The sport captured his imagination. He entered Yale the following year. Tall and slender, he became a star in every varsity sport but favored football.

Camp played for Yale for 7 years, eligibility rules being less strict than today. He captained the football team three years and became its first coach in 1888, though he was an unpaid volunteer. Later he went west to be Stanford's first coach.

He wrote the first national magazine stories and first book on football, popularized the All-American team and for many years was accepted as its sole selector, although the choice was not at first representative since at that time he picked only the eastern players he saw.

Camp pressed for rules that made the sport what it became. It stopped being rugby and became football when he introduced the scrimmage line and the rule requiring the ball to be turned over unless advanced at least 5 yards in 4 downs. He lined off the field at 5-yard intervals.

He campaigned for 11-man teams, created the quarterback position and established the system of numerical signal calling for planned plays. Previously, the coach, who was usually the captain, signalled his teammates with his hands, as do baseball coaches.

From his initial interest, Camp was a prime mover at every major organizational and rules meeting of his sport until his death in 1925. He rightfully is referred to as the Father of American Football. In a sense, he invented the sport.

Originally, it was primarily a kicking game with an almost round ball, which was booted on the run. Camp devised the system of points for scores. Goals kicked following touchdowns were worth 4 points, goals kicked from the field 5 points, safeties 1 point and touchdowns only 2 points when they were accepted in 1883.

The following year the value of touchdowns and safeties was doubled and that of goals after touchdowns halved. In 1898, touchdowns increased to 5 points, goals after touchdown dropped to 1 point. It was not until 1909 that goals from the field settled at 3 points, and in 1912 touchdowns settled at 6 points.

In 1906 the forward pass was legalized, but rules limited it severely and it was not until 1912 that free forward passing was permitted, an end zone established and passes completed in the end zone counted for touchdowns. A year later, passes from Gus Dorais to Knute Rockne popularized passing and Notre Dame football.

By 1881 the field had been reduced to its present dimensions of 100 yards by, curiously, 53 yards. By 1912 the basic unit of possession had been established at 4 downs to gain 10 yards. With passing, the ball began to be reshaped into the narrower ball we know today.

In 1880 teams were limited to 11 players on the field at a time. But substitutions were severely limited until 1932. It was not until 1941 that substituting was permitted so freely that two-platoon football was possible, although there was a recent period from 1953 through 1964 that this again was somewhat limited. Any year now, new limits may be imposed.

In the early years, players wore no padding or helmets; play was so rough and dangerous that by 1905—when a survey showed 18 dead and 159 seriously injured in the sport—it almost was abolished. Columbia did drop the game for a decade and California, Stanford and others abandoned it for a while.

President Theodore Roosevelt saved it in the midseason of 1905 when he brought representatives of the sport from Yale,

Harvard and Princeton to the White House and impressed upon them that it was up to them to reform football or face its gradual disappearance from the scene.

In December of that year, Chancellor Henry McCracken of New York University called a conference of schools participating in football, and they organized into a formal group which 5 years later became the National Collegiate Athletic Association.

The group began to set strict rules for their sport, devise a system of penalties for infractions of proper playing conduct and develop a system of referees and other officials to enforce them.

Gradually the "flying wedge" and other brutal practices disappeared, although the game remains rough. It is still a physical contact sport of blocking and tackling skills originally developed by the pioneer players and teams of the 1880s and 1890s.

Although Rutgers won the first football game, it never has been a national champion and now presumably never will be. Nor did it join the original group of football powerhouses, which did not formally become the Ivy League until 1956. By then the members no longer sought to build national contenders in sports.

Yale, Harvard, Princeton and also Penn were the prime powers in the early years, with Yale outranking the others. They did not always all meet one another and all had a number of undefeated teams, but Yale had more than the others.

In the 28 seasons between 1872 and 1899, Yale's teams won 227 games, lost only 13 and tied 11. The Bulldogs had 18 undefeated teams and 8 that played 5 or more games that went undefeated and untied.

In 1883, the year that a scoring point system was

established, Yale won all 8 of its games and outscored its foes 482-2. It continued in such domination, though occasionally losing or tying a game, until 1887 when it won 9 straight and flailed foes, 515-12.

Still, its first generally recognized national champion was the 1888 club, which was coached by Camp with the aid of his wife, Alice, who conducted practices while her husband worked for a clock company and reported to him so he would be prepared to guide the club in its weekend games.

That team won all 14 of its games and outscored its foes by 704-0. Its stars included Amos Alonzo Stagg, George Woodruff, Pudge Heffelfinger and a bewhiskered captain, Bill "Pa" Corbin.

Stagg, a 27-year-old divinity student, was a star baseball pitcher who became a 157-pound football end, fell in love with the new sport, became a coach, coached longer than any other man ever, invented more wide-open plays than any other man and came to be considered the "grand old man" of the game.

Woodruff was football's first real blocker. He, too, became a coach, one of the first great ones. He coached at Penn for 10 years, from 1892 to 1901, and in one 4-year stretch lost only one of 57 games and claimed 3 national titles.

One of his stars from 1897 to 1900 was Truxton Hare, a 6-2, 200-pounder, who forced his way through foes on powerful legs and has been paired with Pudge Heffelfinger as a guard on the "Early Years All-Stars."

Heffelfinger pioneered the running block. A 6-3, 205-pounder, he was smart, swift and strong and outplayed all opposition. A member of the first All-American team in 1889, he still is regarded as the game's greatest lineman by many experts.

The Minneapolis native became the first pigskin professional when he was paid $500 to play a game in Pittsburgh in 1892. He played on and off for 50 years, and his powerful performance in an exhibition game at the age of 65 awed observers.

It is difficult to determine how good the early stars were by comparison with the modern version, but the bull-like Heffelfinger often said, "A good player would be a good player in any day. Because play was rougher, players of my day were tougher."

They were not as big as modern brutes. Frank Hinkey, who came along to star for Yale in 1891, was only 5-9 and 157 pounds—but he was considered the first ferocious tackler. Called "the greatest player of all time" by the immortal Pop Warner, the spirited, resilient youth starred for teams that compiled 13-0, 13-0, 10-1, and 16-0 records and in two of those seasons outscored their foes by 488-0, and 435-0.

The Poes of Princeton were the most famous players of the early era of that school. A nephew of the poet Edgar Allen Poe sent to the school six sons who played for the Tigers between 1889 and 1900. Three were All-Americans—Arthur, Edgar and John.

Arthur was the best, a brilliant broken-field runner who stole the ball and ran 98 yards to the touchdown that beat Yale in 1898—by 6-0. His most memorable moment came in the Yale game the following year. He was not a kicker, but his team was out of kickers when he volunteered to try for the first field goal of his career. He kicked it from 25 yards out in the last seconds to win the game, 11-10.

They drop-kicked in the early era and Princeton's Alex Moffat was the finest dropkicker of football's first days. He kicked 32 field goals in 15 games, including 6 in one game against Penn, in 1882.

However, the best of all time may have been Pat O'Dea of Wisconsin, who not only was superb as a drop-kicker, but also as a place-kicker and punter in the late 1890s. The Australian-born rugby booter was accurate at 50 yards with dropkicks, booted several from 60 yards out, averaged 85 yards a punt and drove one 110 yards.

O'Dea became coach at Notre Dame. He even was paid for it. John Heisman, who played at both Brown and Penn, commenced coaching at Oberlin in 1892, and may have been the first to be paid, the pioneer professional coach, when he went to Clemson in 1900.

Football had been spreading rapidly to collleges across the country—into the South and Southwest, the Midwest and Far West. Michigan started to play the game in 1879 and 2 years later traveled east to challenge Harvard, Yale and Princeton but lost to all three within six days. Notre Dame debuted in the sport in 1887.

Texas, Texas A&M and Arkansas took up the game in the 1890s. A strong southern team, Sewanee, traveling by train, beat 5 of the best southern and southwestern teams without surrendering a point in six days in 1899. That year Amos Alonzo Stagg coached Chicago to its first Big Ten title.

Someone started to select national champions in 1883, but it is not clear who, nor can any of the early selections be considered seriously. Still, in the last 17 years of the century, Yale is credited with 7 titles and a share of another, Princeton 4 and a share of 1, and Harvard and Penn 3 each.

Princeton had 7 undefeated seasons and 2 undefeated and untied seasons in this period. In one stretch it lost only 3 of 58 games under the coaching of Art Hillebrand. Harvard had 2 undefeated and untied seasons and in one of them, 1890, outscored its foes 555–12. Penn also had tremendous teams.

However, when someone once asked Knute Rockne where his famous shift came from, the Notre Dame coach said, "It came from Yale. Everything in football came from Yale."

Yale early dominated collegiate football in this country, and it is appropriate that the first national champion of consequence came from that school.

That was in 1900. The turn of the century was the turning point for the pigskin sport. The spread of the game across the country and the modernization of the rules were sufficient for kings to be crowned on a reasonable basis from that time on. Crowds of 20,000 or more at contests had become commonplace, and interest in football was flourishing.

In college football the chase for the championship became the base on which an annual attendance of more than 30 million fans has been built. This is rising by about a half million fans each season. Without the big teams and their big games, the polls and other rankings and the controversies that swirl around them throughout the fall and into the winter, week by week, year after year, the sport would be but a shadow of what it is.

3

The First Champions

THE FIRST MODERN national champion in college football clearly was the Yale team of 1900. It was coached by Malcolm McBride, who had just graduated from the school. It was captained by towering Francis "Skim" Brown, who once warned a back that if he fumbled once more he would not play again for Yale. The startled fellow did not fumble again.

Football already was so popular that 85 candidates turned out for the Yale team that year. The best of these was Brown, a rugged guard who with Yale's Hinkey and Penn's Hare became the only 4-time All-Americans in the history of collegiate football. Obviously, most years freshmen have not been eligible to play.

Of the Blue, seven in all were selected to the 1900 All-American team by Walter Camp, who helped coach the club while raising funds for the construction of Yale Bowl. The Blue easily beat its first 8 foes. However, it had a hard time against Columbia before a roaring crowd of 20,000 fans in New York's Polo Grounds.

On the morning of the game McBride found the field had been soaked into a muddy mess by firemen friendly to the host tutor, Foster Sanford, who wanted to slow down the visitors. Columbia had cleated shoes fit to grip the soft surface; Yale did not.

McBride rushed from the arena in search of a shoe store, where he purchased two dozen pairs of shoes with leather soles. Then he sought and found a carpenter who agreed to cut and nail wooden cleats to the soles and deliver everything to the ballpark as soon as possible.

Columbia dominated the first half. Hal Weekes broke loose for a 50-yard run for the first score surrendered by Yale all season. The conversion was missed, but Yale trailed, 5-0, at halftime. The cleated shoes arrived in the dressing room at intermission. Yale found its footing in the second half and rallied to win, 12-5.

In a subsequent game Army was beaten. Then Carlisle. Princeton scored the second touchdown surrendered by that Blue team, but was trounced, 39-5.

That took Yale to a final game, and it was for the national title. The team was unbeaten in 11 games. Arch rival Harvard was unbeaten in 10 games. In fact, Harvard had not been beaten in 3 seasons. And it had a great back in Charley Daly, later a great coach.

But Yale was too tough this time. Inspired by 2 straight losses to the Crimson in previous seasons, the Blue blasted their rival by 28-0 before 22,000 screaming supporters in New Haven. Yale backs rushed for 550 yards in an awesome display of strength.

The traditional Yale victory song, "Boola Boola," was born in the stands that afternoon. It is the Hawaiian term for exaltation, and Yale exalted with the song written by an unknown undergraduate.

The Blue completed the campaign with 336 points to 10 for Yale's foes. Their 12-0-0 record was the only perfect mark among the accepted powers.

Harvard probably was the second best team that season, at least in the East. Penn lost only to Harvard in 13 outings.

Minnesota and Iowa were strong but spoiled each other's records by playing to a tie. Wisconsin lost only to Minnesota by the narrow margin of 6-5.

John Heisman put together a powerful team at Clemson, which won 6 without a loss. Tulane took 5 in a row and blanked its rivals, 105-0. However, in the case of both southern schools schedules were too short and too weak to merit championship consideration.

Harvard claimed a share of the crown in 1901. It won 12 in a row and outscored the opposition, 254-24. Harvard and Yale went into their finale undefeated again, but this time Bill Reid's boys poured it on, 22-0, the worst whipping Harvard yet had handed Yale. Yale also had a tie with Army that year. Cornell upset Penn for the first time but lost one game—by a safety—to Princeton.

One other major team was undefeated, Phil King's Wisconsin club, which won 9 straight and outscored rivals, 317-5. However, it did not meet Michigan, and the Wolverines seem clearly to have been the class of the country in 1901 and entitled to the national title.

Michigan won all 11 starts and blanked its foes by the incredible margin of 550-0. Included was a 128-0 blasting of Buffalo, an 89-0 blasting of Beloit, a 50-0 conquest of Iowa and a 49-0 smashing of Stanford in California in the first Rose Bowl game. Michigan's closest contests were 22-0 defeats of capable Chicago and Carlisle and a 21-0 defeat of powerful Ohio State.

It was the first of 2 straight championships for Michigan's "point-a-minute" team, one of the most famous of all time. In four years the Wolverines won 43 games and tied one and outscored the opposition 2,326 points to 40.

Fielding H. "Hurry Up" Yost, the coach of this incredible club, got his nickname from his zest for speed in every sense.

Standing on the sidelines in practice sessions, he'd holler at his players, "Hurry up, hurry up! Ya think you got all day?"

He was born in a log cabin in Fairview, West Virginia. He was a tough 200-pounder who played at West Virginia and Lafayette. He entered law school but returned to football for a profession instead.

Yost commenced coaching at Ohio Wesleyan in 1897, then shifted in turn to Nebraska, Kansas and Stanford. He put in one-year hitches at each before arriving at Michigan at the age of 31 to settle in. He coached the Wolverines 25 years.

When he retired in 1926 after 29 years of coaching, his record stood at 196–36–12 for an .828 winning percentage. His victories remain among the 10 highest ever, his percentage sixth highest in history. He had 13 undefeated teams, starting with those first 4 at Michigan.

A formal man who wore starched white collars, he was tall, trim, rawboned. He was the model of the fine, old-fashioned football coach. He chewed cigars but never smoked them. He never drank hard stuff. He never cursed. His only real vice was peanuts. He walked around with bags of them. He was very moralistic, a family man, proud of his profession. He was not a great orator but was given to pep talks stressing the new tradition at Michigan.

His first great star, Willie Heston, said of him, "After 50 years studying football, I judge my early coach to be the greatest that ever stepped on a gridiron. He thought about football all but the few hours he slept at night. If you encountered him, you knew he wouldn't let you get away without talking football for hours. He had the sharpest of football minds. He would have made a great general. He made great players and great teams because he would not let young men settle for anything but their best."

Yost himself gave his style of football its famous slogan, "A punt, a pass and a prayer." Actually, it was much more than that. He built his teams around determined defenses, not flashy offenses. He did specialize in the punting game to pin his foes deep. He was the first to favor field position as the critical factor in contests. His teams forced fumbles with their swift, savage tackling. They hurried rivals into making mistakes. They took advantage of scoring chances.

"We were opportunists," he said years later. "But when we got our opportunities we scored. We had all the plays football has had except the pass, and when that came along we put that in, too. There is nothing new in football. You don't fool your foes. You defeat them with execution." He was the forerunner of the Vince Lombardis, who practiced plays to perfection and defeated foes on fundamentals.

His teams ran off plays so swiftly that they kept their rivals off balance and caught them flat-footed. In the January 1, 1902, Rose Bowl inaugural, climaxing the 1901 season, Yost's team ran off 142 plays and rushed for a fantastic 1,463 yards on the ground, totals that may never have been exceeded in a single game. Californians were so shocked that the game was not played again for 14 years, and it was many more years before it was included in the records.

Guard Dan McGugin, shortly to be the South's first famous coach at Vanderbilt, led the Wolverine line charge that day. Quarterback Boss Weeks directed a devastating attack. Neil Snow scored 5 touchdowns. Willie Heston ran for almost 200 yards.

Heston, short and stocky at 5-8 and 184 pounds, was so swift he could outrun national sprinting champion Archie Hahn at 50 yards. He had an explosive start and magnificent moves. Inventive, his most remembered single moment on the playing field came when he literally hurdled Chicago's Walter Eckersall to escape a tackle in the open field one day. But he had many memorable moments, and his 72 touchdowns remain a career record in college annals. Both he and Eckersall have been voted to all-time all-star teams. Later Heston became a lawyer and a judge.

Yost said, "Heston was the most spectacular all-around of all time." Heffelfinger said, "He was the best back who ever lived."

Heston scored 16 touchdowns at "Mee-shee-gan," as Yost always called his school, increased its scoring to 644 points in successfully retaining its national championship in 1902, though it surrendered 12 points this time. Among its 11 straight triumphs were wins by 119-0 over the Michigan Aggies, 107-0 over Iowa, 88-0 over Albion and 86-0 over Ohio State.

However, Wisconsin went down only grudgingly at 6-0. Minnesota and Notre Dame were defeated by 23-0 scores and Chicago by 21-0. It was the only loss suffered by Stagg's Chicago club. Yale also went undefeated, but was tied by Army, 6-6. Yale handed Harvard and Princeton their only defeats. Nebraska at 10-0 and South Dakota at 9-0 also went perfect and outscored their foes by 187-0 and 216-0, respectively, but their rivals were mostly not of championship caliber. However, Nebraska did defeat Minnesota, 6-0.

Minnesota, coached by its first outstanding mentor, Henry Williams, tied Michigan 6-6 to knock the Wolverines from the top spot in 1903. Minnesota won 14 games and Michigan 11 and the tie was the only blemish on either's record. The tie was so vicious that athletic relations were severed for 6 years.

The game was played at Minneapolis and Yost heard a rumor that the Gophers had doped the drinking water provided the Wolverines for the sidelines. He sent his student manager to a local store to buy a water jug and fill it with fresh water, which his players used.

Michigan left it behind. When Minnesota officials sought to renew the rivalry, they pointed out, "We still have your little brown jug. Come up and win it back." Thus one of the first great trophy contests commenced—the annual battle for the "Little Brown Jug," a 30-cent piece of crockery.

Minnesota had an awesome offense that season, scoring 618 points. It surrendered only 12. Michigan scored 565 points and surrendered only the 6 scored by Minnesota. Another team with a record marred only by a tie that year was Notre Dame, which did not permit a point in 9 games, outscoring rivals 292–0, but was held even in a scoreless tussle with Northwestern. Nebraska again was perfect in 10 games.

However, general recognition as national champion in 1903 went to Princeton, which was undefeated and untied in 11 games and unscored on until its final game with Yale. The Tigers scored only 259 points but won a number of close contests from the strongest teams of the time, dealing both Dartmouth and Yale their only losses of the season.

The coach was A. R. T. Hillebrand, who has come to be called Art, combining the three initials he used, or by his nickname, "Doc." The stars were halfback Dana Kafer and guard John DeWitt. The 219-pound DeWitt was a powerful player and brilliant dropkicker.

DeWitt's 50-yard field goal gave Princeton a 5-0 lead against Yale in 1902, but George Chadwick's 2 long runs in the second half dealt Princeton its only loss of that season, 12–5.

DeWitt thirsted for revenge in 1903. Undefeated, favored Yale broke to a 6-0 lead. Then they marched to the Princeton 26-yard-line. Ledyard Mitchell dropped back for a dropkick. DeWitt and the rest of the Tiger line broke through to block it off Mitchell's foot, DeWitt scooped it up and ran more than

70 yards to a touchdown. He added the extra point to tie the game.

Late in the game, he went for a 43-yard field goal from a bad angle. Yale's Tom Shevlin said at the line, "He can't kick it from there." Princeton quarterback Joe Vetterlein replied, "You might as well go home, you've lost." DeWitt dropkicked perfectly for the 11-6 victory. He had scored all the points, and the men from Old Nassau were national champions.

In 1904 Michigan's fourth straight undefeated season qualified it for a share of the title, but it did not meet Minnesota, and the Golden Gophers' seemingly superior record apparently entitled them to claim the crown. Minnesota won 13 straight games, Michigan 11. Minnesota outscored foes by 625-12 to Michigan's 567-22. Michigan beat West Virginia 130-0 and Kalamazoo 95-0. Minnesota beat Grinnell 146-0 and Twin Cities 107-0.

There was not much to choose between the two teams. Michigan beat two top teams, Wisconsin by 28-0 and Chicago by 22-12. Minnesota beat three—Northwestern by 17-0, Iowa by 11-0 and Nebraska by 16-12. Minnesota was a tough team. Its coach, Dr. Harry Williams, a Yale graduate, was an inventive strategist who tutored the Gophers for 22 years but never had a better team than his national-title holders of 1904.

Some say Penn had its greatest-ever team that year and that its 12 straight triumphs, outpointing foes 222-4, entitles it to claim a share of the laurels, too. Another Williams, Dr. Carl Williams, was the coach of this club, and Bob Torrey was the captain and center. But the star was the little quarterback, Vince Stevenson, one of the best ever to play for this school. He was a smart, inspirational leader and a brilliant runner who perfected the straight-arm technique of frustrating tacklers.

Penn had a difficult time defeating such foes as Swarthmore, 6-4, Penn State, 6-0, and Brown, 6-0. It did defeat Harvard 11-0, but did not play Yale. Yale lost to Army that year. Teams that did not lose or tie that year and so could claim a chunk of the crown were Pitt, Vanderbilt, Auburn and St. Louis, but they did not meet the top teams of the time.

However, Vanderbilt coach Dan McGugin and Auburn coach Mike Donohue had begun great dynasties at their schools and developed many teams their supporters believe entitled to titles.

McGugin had played and coached under Yost at Michigan, and he married Yost's sister. He spent his entire 30-year career as a head coach at Vanderbilt, winning 197 games. He once said, "Yost invented everything useful in football, and I was in a position to copy him; how could I miss?"

It was not until 1910 that he proved himself to Easterners when his side visited Yale and fought the favored Bulldogs to a scoreless tie. He sent his southern lads out for blood by telling them, "Men, those Yankees out there are the sons of the men who killed your fathers." It was not until later that they learned McGugin's father had been with General Sherman on his march through Georgia in the Civil War.

Born in Ireland, Donohue played at Yale and coached 32 years. He won 125 games, but most of them came at Auburn, where he ran the show for 19 seasons. From 1913 to 1915 his Tigers put together a string of 21 victories, 2 ties and no defeats.

Maybe the most extraordinary of coaches was Amos Alonzo Stagg, whose Chicago club was considered the champion of college football in 1905. As a divinity student, Stagg got a late start in football. He was born in August of 1862 in West Orange, New Jersey, the son of a shoemaker, and he was 23 when he turned out for football at Yale in 1885. However, he was 92 before he retired from coaching in 1954 and he lived past 100 with his passion for his sport intact.

The short, stocky Stagg coached for 64 years, 55 as a head coach. In that capacity he amassed 314 victories, which endures as the record by one over Pop Warner.

He coached 41 years at Chicago before he was retired in 1933 at the age of 70. "I'm far from finished," the feisty fellow remarked, and promptly went west to the College of the Pacific, where he coached another 14 years with his wife scouting and helping conduct practices. Football was not emphasized at Pacific as it had been at Chicago, where eventually the sport was dropped. However it was working with young men that Stagg preferred to putting together great records.

Retired at Pacific in 1946 at 84, he simply shifted to Susquehanna in Pennsylvania to assist his son, who had become a coach, too. He announced his retirement in 1953 when his wife was sick. "My buddy for 59 years, the best assistant a coach ever had, needs me," he said. But the next year he was back as an assistant at Pacific for one more year.

Stagg did not dissipate and the closest he came to cursing was to call an erring young player "a jackass," which he did quite often. He was determined to "make men of boys," and he insisted it was not football that should matter most to them but their education in college. He did feel they could learn lessons in football and in life as well as in books. An extremely moralistic man, he refused to bend the rules, much less break them, and was known to request a referee to recall a score by his team because one of his players had fouled.

He was a winner because he was incredibly inventive, one of the most imaginative men ever in sports. He developed track techniques and coached Olympic athletes. He invented the overflow trough for swimming pools, which provides calm waters for champions. He invented baseball's batting cage and took a team on the first American tour of Asia.

His contributions to football go beyond counting. He devised more formations and plays that endure than any other single man. His innovations included the huddle, the direct snap from center, the unbalanced offensive line, the flanker backs, the end-around run, the man in motion, the backfield shift, reverses and laterals. He even was the first man to number players' uniforms and the first to award "letters" to his team's players.

When Stagg took over at Chicago as coach in 1892, Benjamin Harrison was president of the United States. Gentleman Jim Corbett had just defeated John L. Sullivan for the heavyweight boxing championship of the world. It was a time few today ever knew, but he was commencing a career that still carries weight today. He made a mark that endures.

The 1905 national championship club was his best. It won all 9 of its games and, though it outpointed its opposition 212–5, it only narrowly nosed out a wonderful Wisconsin team by 4–0 and mighty Michigan by 2–0.

Walter Eckersall was the star, an all-time All-American. In 1900, a prep powerhouse from the East, Brooklyn Poly, went to Chicago to challenge a touted scholastic team there, Hyde Park High. The hosts' Eckersall led a 105–0 rout of the visitors which stunned the spectators, including a youthful gate-crasher named Knute Rockne.

Years later, Rockne said, "I went to the game thinking of football as a pleasant recreation and went home from it thinking of it as a profession. He was my first hero, Eckersall. I was spellbound by his performance and ran on the field to try to touch him afterwards. There were too many others around him, but years later when I played in Chicago, he was the referee and I shook his hand and told him how much he meant to me. He was unsurpassed as a player and inspired me."

Eckersall was only 5-7 and 142 pounds, but he was an imaginative quarterback, a slippery runner, a sure safety man on defense and an incredible kicker. He twice drop-kicked 5 field goals in a single game. And his perfectly placed punts kept Michigan pinned in its own territory during most of the big game of 1905.

Heston was gone, but Michigan remained mighty, led by another all-time All-American, Adolph "Germany" Schulz, a giant at 6-4 and 245 pounds, powerful and as fast as a back, maybe the best center ever. Chicago had won 8 straight games this season, but Michigan had not lost in 57 straight games over 4 seasons. The Wolverines had scored 495 points and not been scored on this season. The climactic contest attracted more than 25,000 fans to Marshall Field in Chicago, which was the top football turnout to that time.

It was Thanksgiving Day, cold but clear. The play was savage. Chicago contained Michigan's overpowering offense, but Schulz and his sizable teammates kept Eckersall under control, too. It became a battle of punters, but Eckersall's long, soaring drives knifing out of bounds near the Michigan goal line kept the Wolverines stymied.

Eckersall tried a dropkick for a field goal from the Michigan 37, but it was blocked. Tom Hammond tried a place-kick from the Chicago 41, but it went wide. Chicago was pinned inside its 10. When Eckersall went to punt from his end zone, Wolverine defenders broke through and seemed certain to block it. Eckersall tucked the ball under his arm, dodged tacklers, darted between the goalposts and circled right to the 22 before he was bounced out of bounds. It saved his side.

Late in the game, Eckersall lifted a high punt into the

Michigan end zone. Instead of touching it down, Denny Clark decided to try to run it out. As he reached the goal line, Chicago's right tackle, Art Badenoch, dove at him and got him low, right end Mack Catlin hit him high and the runner was driven down on his back in the end zone. It was a safety and it won by 2–0 one of the best remembered games of all time and the national championship for Chicago, which concluded with a 212–5 total in points. The only 2 points suffered by the Wolverines all season resulted in their only loss in 5 seasons.

Yale, which won over 10 foes and outpointed them 222–4, also claimed a piece of the crown. Led by fullback Samuel F. B. Morse, and a tremendous tackle, Tom Shevlin, Jack Owsley's Bulldogs did have a hard time with several foes, including Harvard, which the Yale team beat by 6–0. But it won them all.

Penn was unbeaten that season, but tied once. So was Georgia Tech, where John Heisman had taken over. Stanford was undefeated and untied and so, some say, rates a share of the laurels, but it was the first top team from the Far West and was underrated in the East, where honors were handed out. The indications are the Cardinal club could not be compared to Chicago, anyway.

Chicago did not meet Michigan the following year, but was removed from the running for the national title in a 4–2 loss to Minnesota. The midwestern teams took turns knocking each other off. St. Louis, perfect in 11 outings, did not play on the top level. Nor did Utah or Washington State in the Far West, each perfect in 6 starts.

The college championship returned to the East in 1906. Princeton earns recognition here as the leader, although it had a scoreless tie with Yale, and both otherwise were undefeated in 10 games. Yale handed Harvard its only loss, 6–0, beat

Brown by 5-0 and narrowly nosed out Army, 10-6. It out-pointed the opposition, 144-6. The forward pass had just been legalized and quarterback Tad Jones used it effectively at times. Brother Howard played end. Both became great coaches. Tom Shevlin coached this Yale club.

Princeton was somewhat more impressive. It got by Navy, 5-0; Washington and Jefferson, 6-0, and Army, 8-0. It topped a strong Cornell team, 14-5. It outscored rivals, 205-9. Its coach, Bill Roper, who tutored Princeton teams 17 years, was not a master strategist or good at details, but he was an inspirational leader who coined the saying, "The team that won't be beat, can't be beat." Tackle Jim Cooney and end Casper Wister led a Tiger team that was not beaten in 1906.

Yale reclaimed at least a share of the crown in 1907, but Dartmouth appears to be more deserving of the title. Both were undefeated but once tied. Each surrendered only 10 points all season. Yale had a more effective offense, but Dartmouth defeated Harvard more impressively than did Yale, 22-0 compared to 12-0. Yale also had a difficult time defeating Syracuse and Washington & Jefferson by 11-0 scores and Princeton by 12-10.

The Princeton game is one of the great games of football history. Princeton shot into a 10-0 lead at the intermission. Coach Morse's Yale club rallied in the second half on the passing of quarterback Jones and the running of halfback Ted Coy. A remarkable punt return by Jones got the Eli's going. Then Jones's passes set up 2 short runs to scores by Coy that decided the game and sent 35,000 fans into the streets of New Haven shouting happily.

Coy was superb. A handsome blonde looking like a Frank Merriwell come to life, he was a graceful, elusive runner, an accurate dropkicker and punter and a sure blocker and tackler. That season was his first of 3 as an All-American and he unreeled runs of 105 yards against Springfield, 80 against Villanova and 60, 50 and 45 against Holy Cross. He ripped Princeton apart in Yale's dramatic rally.

Against Army, Coy's 70-yard run to set up a possible score was recalled by a penalty or Yale might not have settled for the scoreless tie that marred its record that season.

Jack O'Connor's Dartmouth team was sparked by a pair of splendid linemen, Clarke Tobin and Gus Schildmiller.

Princeton had one of its best teams, but the 2-point loss to Yale and a 1-point loss by 6–5 to Cornell cost it a chance at the championship. Cornell also won over otherwise undefeated Carlisle. Carlisle handed Chicago its only defeat, 18-4, and Penn its only defeat, 26-5. The little Indian school from Pennsylvania, coached by Glenn "Pop" Warner, had an amazing end in the swift, sure Exendine but was developing an even more astonishing star in a freshman named Jim Thorpe. Carlisle was surging into the spotlight.

The only undefeated and untied team of that season was Marquette, which won 6 games far from the spotlight.

The only undefeated and untied teams of the 1908 season were LSU in 11 games and Kansas in 9, but again these schools were so far from the spotlight as to go unrecognized. Not until extensive intersectional competition began to develop over the next few seasons were Deep South and other clubs able to establish their rights to titles.

Carlisle again made a mark in 1908 by putting the only blemish on Penn's record, a 6–6 tie, but the Indians were otherwise erratic and suffered a bad defeat by Harvard among others. Harvard, Penn and Chicago each were unbeaten but once tied. Chicago was tied by Cornell and played only 6 games. Harvard handed Yale its first loss in four years, 4-0. Harvard's only blemish was a 6–6 tie with Navy.

Harvard, led by a mammoth and magnificent tackle, Ham Fish, and in its first year under the coaching of canny Percy Haughton, is entitled to claim part of the crown, but Penn does seem to have been a bit better. Penn won 11 games to 9 for Harvard and scored 215 points to 132 for Harvard. And Penn was especially impressive in a startling 29–0 rout of Michigan. In his only year as coach, Sol Metzger put together a terrific team topped by captain Bill Hollenback at fullback, Hunter Scarlett at end and Dexter Draper at tackle.

Heavy, hard-hitting Hollenback was years later described by Thorpe as his "greatest and toughest opponent." They spent 60 minutes smashing at one another and at the conclusion of the contest both wound up in the hospital to recuperate. Hollenback's greatest game was in the rout of Michigan in which Germany Schulz was injured. "Hollenback hit like a sledgehammer," Schulz sighed.

Although Yale clearly captured only the first and last championships in the first ten years of the new century, it could claim at least a share of 6. And you could not argue about it too strongly if its supporters claimed 3 straight during its unbeaten run from 1905 through 1907. It seems appropriate that it is entitled to the 1909 title at the end of the first decade in modern football.

Yale went undefeated, untied and unscored-on in 10 games. It totalled 209 points, and its only close contest was an 8–0 conquest of Harvard. Captain Coy closed his classic career by drop-kicking two field goals to pace the narrow win over Ham Fish and his Harvard mates in a battle of unbeatens. John Reed Kilpatrick was a destructive force at end on this big day. It was the first national title for coach Howard Jones, who would go on to be the only man ever to win 3 at three different schools.

Arkansas and Washington also were undefeated and un-tied. Another great coach, Gloomy Gil Dobie, was in Washington, putting together the first powerhouse of the second decade, which would go wide open with passing as teams from across the country surged into the title picture.

4

Forward with the Pass

THE FIRST TWO classic championship coaches of the 1900s, Fielding H. Yost and Amos Alonzo Stagg, were moralistic men, but beloved by their players. The next one was not only moralistic, but unloved. Most coaches walk a fine line between being stern and being unreasonable. Gloomy Gil Dobie crossed that line, but he was so successful he endured.

His nickname stemmed from his unsmiling personality and his pessimism. He did not seem to enjoy his job, much less his life, and he talked as if his teams always would lose, the forerunner of many such coaches. His teams seldom lost and, in fact, in his entire nine years as coach at Washington they did not lose once—but he never praised his players.

The slender Scot played without distinction at Minnesota, but copied Michigan's Yost as a coach. Even as the forward pass started to be popular, his teams seldom threw. They ran plays that had been practiced to perfection and often used no more than 9 or 10 plays per game. After one of his teams won a game by 59-7, he put them back on the field to practice because, "those bums can't get away with that performance."

In Seattle, he lived in a small, single room in a private home and it was piled with diagrams. However, sometimes his strategy seemed to consist primarily of brutal off-tackle smashes. His practices always were private. Even former players were barred. When he spoke to his players they were not permitted to speak. He drove them to do more than they thought they could with his stinging sarcasm. "I want machines, not men. None of you have any brains anyway," he once told them.

One of his players said, "If we can take him day after day, we can take anybody on Saturday." His players, the writers and even the fans came to hate him. Spectators in the stands even in Seattle often threw garbage at him, booed him and rooted for his foes, but he was respected for his team's performances. He cursed his critics, commenting, "A football coach can only wind up two ways—dead or a failure."

He seldom failed before he died. He came to Washington from two years as coach at North Dakota Agricultural College and went on to coach at Navy and Boston College for three years and at Cornell for 16. In 33 years his clubs won 179 games, lost 45 and tied 15. Between 1908 and 1916 his Huskies won 58 games, lost none and tied 3, a record unsurpassed by any other single coach at a single school.

He coached 14 undefeated teams in all, including 3 in succession at Cornell, where he became one of the few coaches ever to take national titles at two different schools. Most of his clubs at Washington could have been considered collegiate champions but were not because he scheduled high school and other non-college teams as well as university rivals and few of his foes were regarded highly. Actually, many of the top players in the East and Midwest occasionally played suspect opposition, too, at that time.

Dobie's 1910 team may not have been his best, but it was his second of a series of clubs that ran up a winning streak of 39 games in a row and came in a year when none of the other recognized powers went undefeated and untied. Harvard was undefeated, but tied by Yale. Yale was beaten by Army. Army was beaten by Navy. It was the first of 3 straight Army-Navy games in which Navy failed to score a touchdown, but Army failed to score at all. Navy won all 3 on field goals. Navy did not give up a point in 1910 but was tied scorelessly by Rutgers.

Pittsburgh, which outscored its rivals, 282-0, and Illinois, which outpointed the opposition, 89-0, were unbeaten, untied and unscored on in 9 and 7 games, respectively. Arkansas was unbeaten and untied in 8 games. But in this era no team was as consistently effective and as deserving of a title as Washington, which won 6 games in 1910 and 20 without defeat from 1909 through 1911.

Quarterback and punter Will Coyle, halfback Walt Wand and ends Warren Grimm and Pete Husby were among the top players on Washington's teams of this time.

The western team claimed a share of the crown again in 1911 when it won 7 straight and outscored rivals, 277-7. Oklahoma claimed a share when it won 8 straight and routed rivals, 282-15. But this was the one year out of several outstanding seasons that Carlisle's club seems most entitled to the title despite 1 loss in 12 outings. All the top teams lost or tied games this season. Bill Roper's Princeton team topped Yale and Harvard but tied 2 games, for example.

Glenn "Pop" Warner was as well-liked as "Gloomy Gil" Dobie was disliked. A good guard at Cornell in the early 1890s, Warner coached Georgia to a perfect record in 1896 before returning to his alma mater to coach. He coached two years at Cornell, four at Carlisle, three more at Cornell and eight more at Carlisle before moving on to Pitt, Stanford and Temple. He coached 44 years and won 313 games, figures exceeded only by Amos Alonzo Stagg. Warner's teams lost 106 and tied 32. An Associated Press poll in 1954 proclaimed him "the greatest football coach of all time."

It is said only Stagg was more inventive. Warner's team at

Carlisle in 1897 was the first to wear helmets. He pioneered the spiral pass and spiral punt. He devised the single-wing formation, which was the dominant offensive system until 1940, the double wing, the screen pass, and he developed the reverse play. His teams were tricky and tough.

"I want to win, but I want my boys to have fun, too," he'd say. He was a father figure as well as a coach to his players. He taught them to play hard but clean. His best teams may have been at Pitt when his Panthers won 29 games in a row between 1916 and 1918 to bring him his second national title. His top prominence was achieved at Stanford when he was regarded as the greatest rival to Notre Dame's Knute Rockne as a mentor in the 1930s. But he first shot to the top in his second stint with Carlisle.

Carlisle was a government school set up to teach trades to Indian youngsters. They were recruited off the reservations and most were not of typical college age or education, but many were natural athletes and in good shape from the spartan life they had led.

It was a small school. The football team always lacked reserves, and it had to wander around the country to find foes to play, so it was not able to complete its schedules undefeated and untied, but it surprised and upset most of the prominent teams of the time and was one of the strongest clubs in the country for about ten years.

From the time he returned to Carlisle in 1907, Warner made extensive use of the forward pass, which had just been legalized. Led by Exendine and helped by a newcomer, Jim Thorpe, the Indians lost only to Princeton in 9 starts, handed Penn its only loss and defeated Chicago and Harvard. The next year, a tie with Penn was the only blemish on the latter's record.

Thorpe dropped from school for 2 seasons and the team was

only ordinary, but in 1911 he returned and took the Indians to the top. The following year he returned from the Olympics in Stockholm, where he won the decathlon and pentathlon, to pace the Carlisle club to another splendid season in which it won 12 of 14 games.

Later it was discovered that he had played semi-pro baseball in 1909 and 1910 and his Olympic awards and records were declared void, but an Associated Press poll in 1950 established him as the finest football player of the half-century. The 6-2, 190-pound halfback was an amazing all-around athlete, a fast and powerful runner who averaged 8 yards a run in college, a sparkling kicker and a violent tackler.

He ran for 2 touchdowns in his side's only loss in 1911, to Syracuse. Otherwise, from the time Thorpe scored 17 points in the first 17 minutes of the first game, Carlisle was outstanding. The Indians, with only 16 players, topped top teams, including powerful Pitt by 17-0 and Penn by 16-0. But the big game was against Harvard, undefeated in 8 games.

Harvard led, 6-0, but Thorpe drop-kicked 3 field goals to put Carlisle in the lead, 9-6. Harvard rallied to regain the advantage, 15-9, as the crowd of 20,000 fans roared in Cambridge Stadium. Despite sore legs from an injury that had him on crutches only a week earlier, Thorpe then asked for the ball and rushed it 9 straight times, ripping the Crimson to shreds as he bulled over for a touchdown. He kicked the extra point to tie the contest.

In the gathering gloom, Thorpe kicked a field goal from 50 yards out to score a staggering upset by 18-15 that cemented Carlisle's right to claim the collegiate crown for that year.

The next year Thorpe scored a record 25 touchdowns and 198 points, and Carlisle counted 504 points. The Indians avenged their loss to Syracuse by a 33-0 score and knocked from title contention a strong Army team that included a high-kicking halfback named Dwight David Eisenhower by 27-6. However, a wild defeat by Penn, 34-26, kept Carlisle from keeping the national crown.

The Indians did not get a shot at Harvard, which captured the 1912 laurels with 9 straight victories, although shares of the laurels were claimed by Notre Dame, Wisconsin and Penn State, since each won 7 in a row. Bill Hollenback's Nittany Lions were especially impressive with a 247-6 spread in points, but few in the East felt they were the equal of Harvard.

A former Harvard star, Percy Haughton returned to his alma mater in 1908 to become its most famous mentor. In 9 years there his teams won 64 games, lost only 4 and tied 5. He also coached at Cornell and Columbia, and in 13 seasons he put together a 96-17-6 record for an .832 winning percentage, fourth finest among all coaches of all time.

An aloof man, stern and cold, he drilled his players relentlessly in private practices. He was not an innovator and not above borrowing from more imaginative coaches, but he perfected plays others devised. He once said, "Football is a miniature war game," and he approached his battles with plan and precision. (He later served as a major in World War I.)

He improved his players, and under his direction Eddie Mahan, Tack Hardwick, Ham Fish, Stan Pennock and Charlie Brickley developed into Hall of Famers. Brickley was the star of the 1912 team and Hardwick, Pennock, Sam Felton and captain Percy Wendell were other standouts. Brickley was a great runner and a greater dropkicker. His boot beat Princeton, 3-0, in Harvard's hardest game in 1912.

Yale had humbled Harvard for 6 straight seasons until Haughton took over. The latter's team was held scoreless each time. But the Blue beat the Crimson only once during Haughton's tenure as he restored his school's sporting pride.

In 1912 Yale was undefeated and unscored on until Brickley scored on runs of 60 and 15 yards and two field goals for a 20–0 romp that brought the college crown to Cambridge.

The following year, Brickley drop-kicked 4 field goals and place-kicked 1 for all the points in a 15–5 conquest of Yale that concluded another undefeated season. From late in the 1911 season to midway in the 1915 season Haughton's Harvards went undefeated in 33 consecutive contests, and from 1912 through 1914 the Crimson won 22 straight.

However a second straight perfect season for Notre Dame and the spectacular manner in which it won its games entitled the Fighting Irish to claim their first national title in 1913. Chicago, Michigan State, Auburn, Nebraska and Washington all had perfect records that year, too, as did Harvard and they could claim at least a share of the crown. But, the Irish were brilliant.

1912 stands out in pigskin history as the year in which the fundamental system of 4 downs to advance 10 yards and 6 points for touchdowns was established, and in 1913 Notre Dame moved the sport further toward the modern era by wide use of the up-to-then little-used forward pass, which now could be completed in end zones for touchdowns.

Few realize how early Notre Dame made an impact on football. The South Bend school took up the sport in 1887, and as early as 1901 a team tutored by Pat O'Dea attracted attention with a season in which it lost only 1 game. Two years later Jim Faragher coached the Irish to an unbeaten, un-scored-on season spoiled by a tie. In 1908 and 1909 the Irish lost only 1 game and in 1911, 1912 and 1913 they did not lose any.

John Marks coached the 1911 team—which was tied twice—and the 1912 team, and Jesse Harper took over as tutor in 1913, when the Irish stretched their winning streak to 14 straight games and their unbeaten streak to 25 straight and scaled the summit of their sport. The stars of the team were a fierce fullback, Ray Eichenlaub, a quick quarterback, Gus Dorais, and a swift end, captain Knute Rockne.

Born in Norway in 1888, Rockne was brought to Chicago by his father five years later. Knute practiced sports on the sandlots, but baseball was his game until he was awed by Walter Eckersall's performance. Rockne played high school ball but then had to go to work for four years as a mail clerk, among other things, to save $1,000 to pay for a college education at the University of Illinois.

Had he gone there Illinois might now be the most famous school in football, but when two friends suggested he accompany them to a smaller school, Notre Dame, where it might be easier to get by, Knute was persuaded. However, he recalled being sarcastic about their football teams and being ill at ease as a Protestant within a mostly Catholic student body when he arrived.

Rockne was given a job as a janitor, a good education in chemistry and a chance to play football for a rising power. He soon felt at home under the Golden Dome and developed a lifelong love for his school. "It became my home more than any other I ever was to know," he said, "and football became my life."

He and Dorais, determined that their senior seasons would be the best of 3 straight successful campaigns they enjoyed on the varsity, spent the summer at Cedar Point on Lake Erie, working in the resort restaurant and practicing passing and catching on the beach.

Rockne once said, "I don't know which of us was first captivated by this new weapon, but we both saw tremendous possibilities in it and, once it was freed by changes in the rules, our coach agreed it would be wise to work on it as much as possible. It was work, too, because Dorais had to learn how to pass the pigskin properly, and I had to learn how to catch it without either of us knowing what we were doing."

They improved rapidly and helped their side sandwich slaughters of Ohio Northern by 87-0 and Alma by 62-0 around a 20-7 setback handed them by stubborn South Dakota before arriving at West Point for the fourth game of their season. Notre Dame remained largely unknown. One newspaper referred to the Hoosiers as a school "from Illinois." An awesome Army team was heavily favored. Only 3,000 fans assembled in the wooden stands, although admission was free.

It would become the most famous single game of all time.

On its second offensive series, Eichenlaub's line smashes helped Notre Dame to the Army 25-yard line. From there the diminutive Dorais lobbed the ball to the agile Rockne in the end zone for the first score on the surprised Cadets.

Army marched right back, completing a pass of its own before its backs bulled over to tie. Notre Dame could not move the ball, and when Army got it back it marched again. With the help of a penalty the Cadets smashed a score over on the sixth try from the 1 to take a 13-7 edge as the anticipated rout appeared to be on.

Aerial lightning struck here, however. A pass to Joe Pliska for 30 yards and one to Rockne for 35 yards, the longest completion in history at that time, helped the Irish back to a 14-13 lead leaving the writers and spectators stunned at intermission.

The third period was scoreless. Army reached the Irish 2, but failed on three tries, one when Rockne made a tremendous tackle, another when Dorais intercepted a pass in the end zone. The Cadets were done.

Notre Dame started to fill the air with passes, which

confounded their foes. When the Cadets fell back to defend, Eichenlaub and other runners ripped through the weakened defenses for long gains. Notre Dame scored 3 touchdowns in the fourth period to complete a 35-13 rout in the first of many great Army–Notre Dame games.

The Irish completed 13 of 17 passes for 243 yards. *The New York Times* called it "sensational football." It reported, "The Army players were hopelessly confused and chagrined. Their style of old-fashioned play was no match for the spectacular attack of the Indiana collegians." The report concluded, "Football men marvelled at this startling display of open football."

It was Army's only loss of the year. But Notre Dame went on to whip Penn, Christian Brothers College of St. Louis and Texas to take the national title, its first of many.

Rockne and Dorais had graduated and Army avenged itself the next year. Yale beat the Irish, too, but the mere fact it agreed to play Notre Dame made the game a milestone. For the next four years Notre Dame lost only 1 game each year, but it was not until Rockne had returned as coach that the Irish reached the top again.

Army adopted the passing offense, and Charley Daly's club completed an unbeaten season in 1914. But Bob Zuppke's Illinois squad also went unbeaten and appears to have stopped stronger foes, including Minnesota, Wisconsin, Ohio State and Chicago.

Bert Macomber, a fine field general and accurate kicker, was the playing star as Illinois won 7 straight, but the brilliant, Berlin-born Bob Zuppke was the team's best asset. A former Wisconsin player who coached Illinois from 1913 through 1941, the durable, dynamic coach was an easy-going, fun-loving fellow who lost a lot of games. However, he won more than he lost and always seemed able to win the ones he wanted the most when he put his mind to it and got his boys to bear down. He became "master of the upset," who spoiled many a season for the top teams.

Texas, Tennessee and Washington & Lee also were undefeated and untied that season, and Auburn was undefeated and unscored on, but twice tied. The next season, Cornell, Pitt, Nebraska, Oklahoma, Washington and Washington State all were undefeated and untied. Top teams from all sectors of the country were starting to attain the limelight.

Al Sharpe's Cornell club claimed a share of the 1915 crown with 9 straight triumphs, including routs of Michigan and Penn and handed Harvard its only loss. Harvard bounced back to deal Yale its worst-ever loss with marvelous Eddie Mahan scoring 29 points in a 41-0 romp. Nebraska dealt Notre Dame its only loss—by 1 point. However, Pitt appears to have had the most powerful club of this season.

This was Pop Warner's first Pitt team and the first of 4 straight undefeated and untied teams that would run up the sixth longest winning streak of all time, 31 games, and bring him his second and third national titles and the right to claim others. Clearly, it was one of the classic clubs of all time.

It was a smart team and among its stars trained by Warner who became outstanding coaches were Jock Sutherland, Tiny Thornhill and Red Carlson. The top players were a super center, Bob Peck, and a powerful fullback, George McLaren. The most difficult game was a 14-7 conquest of Penn and the most impressive a 47-12 rout of Navy.

The latter may have been a mistake. Although Pitt, with what Warner and others feel may have been the best team of all time, could claim the crown again in 1916, an aroused Navy team scored the only points permitted by Pitt all season and the Panthers so narrowly escaped with a 20-19 nod that it may have cost them the title.

Army's more decisive 15-7 conquest of the Middies earns the Cadets recognition as champions for that season. Army, which claimed a share of the 1914 crown, was even more outstanding in 1916. This, too, was a club which turned out classic coaches. Charley Daly's roster included Bob Neyland and Biff Jones.

However, the hero was Elmer Oliphant, a small, but sturdy all-around athlete of amazing skills. He won 17 letters in football, baseball, basketball and track at Purdue and was also a diving champion. Suffering from a broken ankle in one football game he kicked a field goal to beat Illinois. Knocked down in a basketball game, he shot in the winning basket against Illinois while seated on the court. He still holds hurdling records set on grass courses.

Eligibility requirements being loose in those days, he was permitted to play at West Point when he accepted an appointment to the Military Academy, and he became the first four-sport letterman there. He was on his way to the All-Time All-American team in 1916 when he set enduring records at Army of 6 touchdowns and 45 points in a 69-7 rout of Villanova.

The 5-7, 174-pound Oliphant kicked 2 field goals in the only loss allowed by Notre Dame all season, 30-10. He scored on 80 and 90 yards in a 53-0 rout of Trinity. And he had runs of 50 and 80 yards, a touchdown and a field goal in a 15-7 defeat of Navy to wrap up a 9-0-0 championship campaign for the Cadets.

Much of the season Harry Williams' Minnesota team was regarded as the best. Bulwarked by Bert Baston, the Gophers averaged 60 points in their first 4 games. Walter Camp called them "the perfect team." He and other national correspondents assembled to see them play against Illinois, a 40-point underdog.

Bob Zuppke instructed his team to kick off flat, sending the pigskin spinning. Minnesota backs fumbled it before falling on it on their 5. Teams seldom scouted foes in those days, but Zuppke had charted the Gophers and knew that they gave the ball to the same 3 backs on the first 3 plays of every game. He ordered his defenders to tackle them in that order, ignoring others. If Minnesota ran others, he'd take the blame. They did not and the Gophers were stopped cold.

They punted to midfield and Zuppke unveiled a new offensive formation with all 11 players spread across the field and no backs in sight until they shifted into position just before the snap of the ball. They marched right through a dumbfounded Minnesota team to score. Minnesota tried to regroup, but Zuppke put his players into unorthodox defenses. Illinois intercepted a pass and scored again.

Illinois won, 19-14, in what still is said to be the biggest upset in college football history, but only one of many surprises sprung by Zuppke.

A title claimant from the Midwest that did not meet Minnesota that year was Ohio State, which had a perfect 8-game slate—its first such—for its first Western Conference crown. The next year it was undefeated, but tied once. John Wilce's superb squad was spearheaded by Chic Harley, who in 1916 won the big games for the Buckeyes by returning 2 punts for touchdowns in defeat of Wisconsin and ran for the touchdown and place-kicked the extra point from a difficult angle to beat Illinois, 14-13. In those days conversions came from the point the goal line had been penetrated.

High school football was king in Columbus when Harley arrived to become its brightest scholastic star. His East High team did not lose a game until its last game. Curiously, his Ohio State teams did not lose a game until his last game when he returned from a year at war to conclude his career in 1919.

A 155-pounder with super skills and an appealing personality, he was the most popular player in Columbus history and made Columbus a college football town. His exploits started the Scarlet and Grey on its way to the top in his sport.

The top team in the East was Brown, which, led by Fritz Pollard, the first great black star in college football history, scored twice in each of 2 startling upsets of Yale and Harvard. But the best team in Brown history lost a claim on the crown when upset by Washington State, 14-0, in the first renewal of the Rose Bowl classic.

The top team in the South was Georgia Tech, which set the all-time college football record score with a 222-0 slaughter of small Cumberland, but for a second straight season had a perfect record ruined by a tie. Georgia Tech attained the top spot the following season with a 9-0-0 campaign.

John Heisman, who played at Brown and Penn, was the original "gypsy coach." He coached for 36 years from 1892 to 1927 at Oberlin, Akron, Clemson, Penn, Washington & Jefferson and Rice, as well as at Georgia Tech, and won 185 games, more than 70 percent of his games. After retirement he became athletic director at New York's Downtown Athletic Club which named the "player of the year" trophy for him.

Watching a Georgia punter throw to a teammate in desperation under a rush in 1895, a play the referee ruled legal, Heisman turned it into a planned play and so invented the forward pass. He also turned up with the hidden-ball trick in which a runner secreted the ball under his jersey, but this later was outlawed.

A Shakespearean actor at times, he had a dramatic, rigid personality. He would not let his players wash with soap and water, because he was convinced it softened their skin. They may have been soiled, but many of them were the best, blessed by his imaginative offenses.

One of the best backfields ever—Everett Strupper, Albert Hill, Judy Harlan and the great Joe Guyon, an Indian "gypsy" who had played with Jim Thorpe at Carlisle—led the Rambling Wreck to victories by 98-0 over Carlisle, 83-0 over Vanderbilt, 41-0 over Penn and 68-7 over Auburn. Auburn spoiled Ohio State's perfect season; Pitt barely beat Penn, 14-6; so Georgia Tech rated the top spot.

Aside from Georgia Tech and Pitt, Texas A&M, Washington State and Denver also put up perfect records that season.

The next year, 1918, was a war year in which many colleges did not compete or played curtailed schedules. Pitt again went unbeaten and untied, as did Texas and Virginia Tech. Pitt played only 4 games. But Pop Warner's powerful Panthers reclaimed the laurels with a 32-0 rout of another strong Georgia Tech team, which won 1 game by 128-0 and totalled 462 points that season but didn't score in the big one. Pitt did lose to the Cleveland Naval Reserve 11-9, but it was discounted because the latter was not a college club.

As World War I ended and the sport resumed in earnest, it entered the Knute Rockne era, when the game became glamorous.

5

The Rockne Era

OF ALL THE men most closely identified with football, the one man who did the most to popularize the sport was Knute Rockne. He typified the "Spirit of Notre Dame" and of football and boosted the school to the top in the sport—and the sport to the top in the imagination of the public. He made a mark that endures.

A short, balding man with a bashed-in nose, the Rock looked like a losing prize-fighter from the past. But he was a brilliant, witty, charming man and a clever coach and inspirational leader. An orator of the first rank, he had that curious quality which caused men to listen to him, believe in him and follow him.

As a student, Rockne majored in chemistry and his grades were always above 90. Graduating in 1913 after he had helped put the pass in the game with his school's stunning upset of Army, he became a chemistry teacher and an assistant coach. At the age of 30 he succeeded Jesse Harper as head coach in 1918 and continued through the 1930 season.

Rockne was killed in a plane crash in an Iowa cornfield shortly after his forty-third birthday in March of 1931. His premature death was mourned world-wide.

Knute Rockne was the first football man whose fame extended beyond the borders of this country. Rockne inspired the rise of his sport in the 1920s, the "Golden Decade" of football, when crowds at contests first started to exceed 50,000 regularly. A Notre Dame–Southern Cal game in Soldier Field, Chicago, attracted 110,000 fans and grossed a half-million dollars at the gate.

By now he seems more myth than man, but those who were there testify to the truth of the tales told of him. His teams were small, but speedy and deceptive and blessed by brilliant talents. He took good players and made them great. He took good teams and made them great. He plotted superb game plans and put passion in his players with his pep talks. Before games, he spoke emotionally until his tigers were ready to tear rivals to shreds. Other times he tried other tactics.

There was the time his Notre Dame team was losing at halftime. While his players waited for him to tongue-lash them, the Rock sat in silence throughout the intermission. Finally, he said, simply, softly, "The Fighting Irish—bah!" Another time when the Irish were losing at halftime, Rockne did not even enter the dressing room until it was time to return to the field. Then he stuck his head in the door and said, "Let's go, girls." Stung, his teams responded with rallies to win both times.

Perhaps in a less sophisticated time his tactics worked where they would not today. But Rockne was a man for his time and when he asked his players if they "wanted to be the first Notre Dame team to be a bunch of quitters," he was in his way making sure they would not be. And they were not; they won.

He once said, "Football is a game of emotion. If you run faster and hit harder than the other guys, you are going to win. It's my job to make my men run faster and hit harder than the other teams. When we do, we win. It's a great job, especially when you win. It's a great game because it can bring out the best in a man. It's my life and it's been a great life working with great young men at a great school."

Rockne created a tradition at Notre Dame which has not died. "The Victory March" remains the most revered fight song in football. Losing only a dozen games in 13 seasons as head coach from 1918 through 1930, the Rock's teams ran up 105 victories, 12 defeats and 5 ties for an .897 winning percentage, which never has been surpassed in the sport.

His teams won 34 of 35 games at one point and 21 of 22 at another point, had one winning streak of 20 games and, at the time of his death, another of 19. He won or shared in 5 national titles with 5 undefeated and untied seasons, the first of which came in 1919 when his Irish wrapped up 9 victories in a row.

That 1919 Notre Dame team included some of the most colorful characters in the history of the sport—George Gipp, Clipper Smith, Hunk Anderson, Eddie Anderson, Buck Shaw, Dutch Bergman, Slip Madigan, George Trafton and others. Gipp was the star, termed by the Rock the greatest player he ever had.

A handsome young man and a great all-around athlete, Gipp had a weakness for gambling, girls and dissipation. An award-winning ballroom dancer, he was hooked on cards and pool, but he gave his winnings away. Fun-loving, he didn't take life seriously. It was hard not to love him, even though he tested the patience of more dedicated men.

Rockne once observed, "If he'd put everything he had into football, he'd have been the best back ever." As it was, he ranks as one of the best. Rockne spotted him spiralling 60-yard punts in street shoes while fooling around with pals on the practice field. Rockne asked him why he wasn't out for football. Gipp said because he was on scholarship to play basketball and baseball.

"Are you afraid of football?" Rockne asked.

"Me, afraid?" Gipp snorted.

"Oh, you're tough," Rockne sneered.

"As tough as I need to be," Gipp replied.

Challenged, Gipp turned out for the team—and turned out to be as tough as he had to be. That was in 1917 and he drop-kicked a field goal 68 yards to win a game for the freshmen. Gipp broke a leg and dropped out of school, but returned in 1919 to lead the Varsity's march to a national title. He sparked a comeback from 0-9 to a 12-9 triumph over Army that sealed the laurels.

Dana X. Bible's Texas A&M team and Charley Moran's Centre team also were undefeated and untied that year, but did not face foes the equal of Notre Dame's. The Texas Aggies were unscored on in both 1917 and 1919, outpointing the opposition 270-0 and 275-0. Balding, biblical, scholarly, Bible won 198 games in 33 years as a coach at Mississippi, LSU, Nebraska, Texas A&M and Texas.

A conservative strategist, he was the first coach to concentrate on scouting and simply was better prepared than his rivals. He produced the first outstanding teams in the Southwest to be accorded national recognition. Some claim the crown for his 1917 and 1919 clubs, but they were not tested outside their sector in intersectional competition. In 1920 the Aggies were upset by Texas, which went undefeated and untied.

Harvard was undefeated in both 1919 and 1920, but tied by Princeton both seasons. Chic Harley led Ohio State to a perfect record in 1920 until they were upset by the master of the upset, Bob Zuppke and his Illinois team, in the season finale, 9-7. The next season Harley's Buckeyes were unbeaten until clobbered by California in the Rose Bowl.

Gipp gave Notre Dame another undefeated season in 1920.

He ran and passed for 332 yards in a 27-17 triumph over Army. Two weeks later he suffered a cracked collarbone and dislocated shoulder against Indiana, but he returned late in the game to run, pass and kick "Rockne's Ramblers" from an 0-10 deficit to a 13-10 victory.

One week later, suffering from the flu, he left a sick bed to accompany the team on a trip to Northwestern. Rockne never forgave himself for allowing Gipp to talk himself into the game. Gipp starred in a 33-7 romp, but chill winds which blew across the icy field aggravated his sickness. He was sent back to bed, but died of pneumonia the next month.

California—not Notre Dame—generally is regarded as the college champion of 1920. Andy Smith's "Wonder Team" scored twice as many points as the Irish in routing rivals, 510-14. The Bears claimed the crown after concluding the campaign with a startling 28-0 romp over previously undefeated Ohio State in the Rose Bowl the following New Year's Day.

Big Brick Muller, a 6-2, 215-pound end who not only caught passes but threw them, was the star of the Bears, the first far-western All-American and an all-timer. An Olympic silver-medalist in the high jump and a sprint star, the magnificent Muller's 55-yard pass to Brodie Stephens, the longest scoring toss of its time, started the rout of Ohio State and was the first famous Rose Bowl play.

Charley Erb quarterbacked the title team, which went on to claim at least a share of another crown in 1922 when it also went undefeated and untied. The Bears were undefeated but once tied in 1921 and 1923. Muller never played in a losing game in college. After graduation, he became an outstanding orthopedic surgeon.

After he left, the 1924 Cal club put together one more undefeated season, but it was twice tied. The fifth straight undefeated season was the highlight in the career of Andy

Smith, less an innovator than a perfectionist, who prepared his teams meticulously. An All-American fullback on an undefeated team at Penn in 1904, Smith coached for 17 seasons at Penn and Purdue, as well as at Cal, with a winning percentage above .760 at the time of his death in 1925.

Another outstanding team of 1920 was the Boston College club, which was undefeated that year and again in 1926 under the coaching of Frank Cavanaugh, who went on to war heroics and became famous as "The Iron Major." Cavanaugh coached 138 victories at Fordham, Holy Cross, Dartmouth and Boston College, but his 2 Boston teams were the only 2 to claim shares of the college crown.

The 1921 title went to Iowa, largely on the basis of a 10–7 upset of Notre Dame to end a 20-game winning streak for the Irish. One of the first black stars in football and one of the great tackles of all time, swift, strong Duke Slater, led a defense that dominated captain Eddie Anderson and the rest of Rockne's crew. Aubrey Devine's 38-yard dropkick field goal finished off the Irish, who won 10 other games.

The Hawkeyes beat the best in the Midwest on a 7-game schedule to net Yaleman Howard Jones his first college crown.

Others lodged claims to the crown. California won 9 in a row before a scoreless tie with Washington & Jefferson in the mud in the Rose Bowl. Asked about Washington & Jefferson before the game, a Cal player had said, "All I know about them is they're both dead." But Earle "Greasy" Neale's Presidents topped Pitt that season and also were perfect except for that tie. It was Washington & Jefferson's best season, although its greatest star, the immortal tackle Wilbur "Fats" Henry already had graduated.

Jock Sutherland's Lafayette team, unbeaten and untied that season, also beat Pitt, which led the Panthers to secure Sutherland as their coach.

Uncle Charley Moran's Centre College club contended for the laurels until defeated by Dana X. Bible's Texas A&M team in the Dixie Classic, the forerunner of the Cotton Bowl, 22–10. The little Kentucky club, nicknamed the "Praying Colonels" because of their pregame prayers, threw more than a prayer against Harvard at Cambridge before 45,000 stunned spectators. A 33-yard scoring run by Bo McMillin made him and the school forever famous.

He darted through a hole in the right side, cut untouched to the left sideline, stopped in his tracks at the 10 as two startled tacklers angling in on him flew past, started again and dragged a third tackler across the goal line. It was the only score of an upset that some say is the most incredible ever.

Gloomy Gil Dobie's Cornell club compiled a perfect record in 8 starts at the beginning of a string of 24 consecutive victories over 3 perfect seasons. Its biggest triumph in 1921 was a 41–0 pounding of Penn, despite a muddy field, as Eddie Kaw scored 5 touchdowns on runs of 5 to 45 yards. Kaw and George Pfann were the stars of that team, which returned to win 9 more in a row in 1922. Pfann, who went on to Oxford, a brilliant legal career and awesome Army accomplishments, was the smart, quick quarterback of the team, Kaw the breakaway runner. Kaw was small and slow, but elusive, with a tricky, twisting style of running that frustrated tacklers.

Pfann and Kaw did not lose a game in the 2 seasons they were teamed. After Kaw graduated, Pfann quarterbacked his third straight perfect season. In these 3 seasons, Dobie's Cornell clubs totalled more than 1,000 points. The best of the 3 seasons came with the 1922 club, which can be considered champions of that college campaign. The upstate New Yorkers routed most rivals and turned back vengeful Penn, 9–0, in their only close call. Cornell did not meet Princeton that season, however, and Princeton and Cal also compiled perfect records.

Bill Roper's Princeton Tigers of 1922 came to be called the "Team of Destiny" because it somehow squeezed past foe after foe in one close contest after another. Its closest call came in Chicago before 32,000 fans—and more listening to the first radio broadcast of a game. Amos Alonzo Stagg's Maroons mounted an 18-7 lead and had Princeton pinned on its 1-yard line early in the final period. From punt formation, Johnny Gorman gambled and passed 40 yards to Jack Cleaves to put the Tigers in good field position. A little later Chicago regained the ball, but Howdy Gray scooped up a fumble and ran 42 yards to a touchdown. Ken Smith's conversion cut the deficit to 18-14. With time running low, Cleaves passed to Smith for 25 yards and Willie Wingate for 15, and Harry Crum crashed over to put Princeton on top. Smith's kick made it 21-18.

Chicago charged back to a first down on the Princeton 7 with 1 minute left and madness erupting in the arena. Jarring John Thomas, the powerful fullback, smashed into the line 4 straight times. The Tigers stopped him 4 straight times, inches from the goal line the last time, and the "Team of Destiny" had gained its greatest triumph, one which entitled it to claim part of the crown for that year.

The Ivy League had two teams with perfect records in 1923, as did the Western Conference. Cornell nosed out Penn, 14-7, and routed all other rivals in completing its string of three great years, but did not meet Yale. The Yale team of Tad Jones was one of the greatest in Eli history, but barely beat Maryland, 16-14.

A fantastic 55,000 filled Harvard's Soldier Field to see the Crimson test the Blue. Tad told his team, "Gentlemen, you are about to play for Yale against Harvard. Never will you do anything so important!'' For the first time since 1916, Yale beat Harvard, 13-0, as Ducky Pond ran 67 yards to score with a fumble and "Memphis Bill" Mallory kicked a conversion and a couple of field goals. Other stars of that team were Century Milstead and Mal Stevens.

Fielding Yost's Michigan team, deprived of its title shot by a tie the previous season, put together a perfect record this season. Harry Kipke, a super punter, paced an eleven that permitted only 1 touchdown. Though once tied, Cal permitted only a single touchdown, too—as did SMU, also unbeaten and untied. But the class of the campaign appears to have been Bob Zuppke's Illinois team, which overcame awesome opposition.

The Illinois star was sophomore Red Grange, who broke in by galloping off 3 scoring runs in 39 minutes as Illinois won by 24-7 over a Nebraska team that would be the only one all year to top Notre Dame. He turned end twice on long sweeps to set up a short run for the only touchdown in a 7-0 conquest of Chicago for that club's only loss of the year. His 92-yard touchdown dash defeated Northwestern, 9-6.

The slender, but sturdy, swift and elusive Grange ran 44, 56, 67 and 95 yards to 4 touchdowns in 12 minutes to hand Michigan its first defeat in 3 years in 1924; and 15, 55 and 60 yards to 3 touchdowns at Penn in 1925 that dazzled the East. However, "The Galloping Ghost," who glamorized college football, never again starred on as solid a team as Illinois's 1923 national titleholders.

He ran for 31 touchdowns and 3,600 yards in his spectacular college career and went on to promote the pros to prominence.

It sometimes seemed no one man could match him. In 1924, even as Grange was starring at Illinois, it took four men to top him at Notre Dame. They took the national title for Rockne's Ramblers. They were Harry Stuhldreher, Don Miller, Jim Crowley and Elmer Layden. Not one of them weighed as much as 165 pounds, but they were swift and smart and performed flawlessly in the "Notre Dame Shift," which Rockne introduced that year. The backs shifted from one offensive formation to another a split-second before the defense could adjust. It was not until the rules later were revised, forcing the famed four to stop before the snap of the ball, that they could be contained.

Put together in midseason of the year before, quarterback Stuhldreher and his three running backs reached their peak in 1924 and outran all rivals. They attained immortality in the third game of the season when they whipped Army, 13–7, before 55,000 fans in New York. The greatest of sportswriters, Grantland Rice, led off his story for the next day with the following lines:

> Outlined against a blue-gray October sky, the Four Horsemen rode again. In dramatic lore they are known as famine, pestilence, destruction and death. These are only aliases. Their real names are Stuhldreher, Miller, Crowley and Layden. They formed the crest of the South Bend cyclone before which another fighting Army team was swept over the precipice at the Polo Grounds this afternoon.

The next day, Bill Fox of the *Indianapolis News* asked George Strickler, whom the promotion-minded Rockne had made the first publicity director in college sports, for a picture of the four atop horses. The photo and story have been reprinted regularly ever since and the "Four Horsemen" never will be forgotten.

77

They might have been had they failed later, but they did not. Crowley ran for 250 yards as Notre Dame returned to the East to top Princeton, 12-0. The Tigers never again scheduled the Irish. Georgia Tech, Nebraska and Wisconsin were walloped. Miller ran 30, 60 and 88 yards for scores against the Engineers. Layden returned an interception 45 yards to score as Northwestern was subdued, 13-6. Carnegie Tech held the Irish even at 13-13 for a half at Forbes Field, Pittsburgh, but Stuhldreher completed 19 passes in the second half to spark a 40-19 runaway.

Rockne accepted a postseason invitation for the first time in Notre Dame history, and his team went to the Rose Bowl to oppose Pop Warner's undefeated Stanford team, which starred one of the most brilliant backs ever, Ernie Nevers. The 210-pound fullback savaged the "Seven Mules," as the great Notre Dame line had come to be called, for more than 100 yards, but was stopped several times in the shadow of the goal line. Layden uncorked two 80-yard punts to pin the Indians deep in their territory, then intercepted passes and returned them on touchdown runs of 55 and 60 yards. The Irish prevailed, 27-10.

Notre Dame has had better teams than that of 1924, but it had no competition for the national title that year and no club ever became better known. It did not again risk its great records in postseason bowl games for 45 years and thus deprived selectors of a valuable yardstick in crowning college kings. (The Big Ten also held out against postseason play.)

Alabama gained the championship in 1925, earning the right by proving itself in a dramatic 20-19 conquest of undefeated Washington in the Rose Bowl.

Johnny Mack Brown, a great receiver and runner, who later became a cowboy star in films, sparked the team to 10 consecutive triumphs. Coach Wallace Wade was a master of defense, and his team permitted only 1 touchdown until the last game. Offensively it scored almost 300 points, including 20 in 6 minutes in the second half to rally from a 13-point deficit to a 1-point win. Washington had scored more than 450 points. Its star, George Wilson, accounted for more than 200 yards in this classic contest. But the Deep South emerged with the national title, its first of several in this period.

Jess Hawley's Dartmouth team, led by Swede Oberlander, trimmed 8 foes and routed such powers as Cornell by 62-13 and Chicago by 33-7, but met neither the "Big Three" of the Ivy group, nor any top teams in postseason play. Fielding Yost's Michigan team, which he regarded as the strongest of his career, had a great passer, Benny Friedman, and a great end, Benny Oosterban, and did not surrender a single touchdown all season, but had the season marred by a 3-2 loss to Northwestern. Clark Shaughnessy's unbeaten Tulane team was stymied by a tie with Missouri.

Outside of little Lafayette, the undefeated and untied teams in the country as the 1926 campaign came toward a close were Notre Dame, Navy, Alabama and Stanford. Rockne was so sure the Irish could clobber Carnegie Tech in their closer that he went to see Navy play Army instead. It was what he later termed the "greatest mistake" of his career. Notre Dame beat Navy early the next year, but by then Carnegie Tech had upset the Irish, coached by aide Hunk Anderson, 19-0.

Well, everyone wanted to see Army-Navy in 1926. The crowd, 110,000 in Soldier Field, Chicago, was a record for college competition. The classic series, started in 1890, has never had a more spectacular contest. Navy had handed Michigan its only loss of the season. Army had lost only 1 game all season. Favored Navy sailed into a 14-0 lead, but Army, led by brilliant backs Chris Cagle and Harry "Lighthorse" Wilson rallied to tie at 14-14.

Early in the second half, Cagle broke free and sprinted 43 yards to put the Cadets on top, 21–14. After that, the Cadets turned back bids by the Middies again and again until late in the game. Trying to retain possession of the ball, an Army aerial was intercepted by Alan Shapley. Behind the blocking of a great tackle, Frank Wickhorst, Navy drove deep. Shapley ran in from the 8 on a double-reverse that dazzled Army. The roar of the crowd hushed as All-American halfback Tom Hamilton prepared to kick the conversion. It was perfect, producing a thrilling tie.

After Alabama and Stanford tied, 7–7, in the Rose Bowl, the general feeling was that of the several unbeaten, once-tied powers, Navy most merited the national title.

Others with similar records that year were St. Mary's, SMU and Brown. That was the only undefeated season ever for Brown, coached by Tuss McLaughry. Tied by Colgate in the last game of the 1926 campaign, Brown had 3 straight strong teams at that time in which its 11 starters played 60 minutes of almost every game. NYU, coached by Chick Meehan and sparked by Ken Strong, also had 3 straight strong teams at that time, but slipped one way or another each year.

Again, not a single top team had a perfect record in 1927. Notre Dame lost to Army. Army beat Navy but lost to Yale. Yale lost to Georgia. Georgia lost to Georgia Tech. No one was able to go undefeated and untied. Minnesota had the bruising Bronco Nagurski but was twice tied. Illinois was tied by Iowa State. Texas A&M was tied by Texas Christian.

Of them all, Dana X. Bible's Texas Aggies seem most deserving of the laurels in 1927. They outscored rivals by 222 points to 32. They knocked off an undefeated Southern Methodist team by a startling 39–13. In that game, an Aggie immortal, 145-pound Joel Hunt, a tiny terror, scored 3 touchdowns and passed for a fourth, intercepted a pass and punted for a 40-yard average. The captain and signal-caller, he was also the team's place-kicker and fiercest tackler. He missed only 3 minutes of action all season, one of many brilliant ones for Bible's boys and the first to merit national title recognition for a squad from the Southwest.

During the next 2 years 2 more southern teams earned national championships. In all, 5 southern schools claimed the college crown in the 7 seasons from 1925 through 1931.

In 1928, Georgia Tech, led by powerful tackle Peter Pund, had the only undefeated and untied team in the country, but by only the sheerest of margins. After concluding their campaign with a 13-0 victory over Notre Dame, the Engineers entered the Rose Bowl game against a California team that had succeeded with a scoreless tie in spoiling a perfect record for Southern Cal.

The classic was scoreless in the second period. Georgia Tech's Stumpy Thompson fumbled when tackled by Benny Lom. The ball bounced into the hands of the California captain and center, Roy Riegels, who got turned around in the scramble and started to run the wrong way from his own 35-yard-line toward his own goal line. The confused crowd was roaring. One of the few who was not confused, Lom, ran after Riegels, hollering to him to stop. He slowed down. Lom caught hold of Riegels' hand and turned him around at the 1. Tech tacklers, trailing him, hit him down then. Riegels, who had thought he was running for a touchdown, arose and stood there stunned as the realization of his error reached him.

Lom tried to punt out of trouble, but Tech tackle Vance Maree blocked it. It deflected off a Cal player out of the end zone for a safety and a 2-0 Tech edge. Georgia Tech's Tommy Thomason built the advantage to 8-0 in the third period. Riegels blocked a Tech punt to launch a rally. It concluded with a scoring pass from Lom to Irv Phillips. A conversion kick by Barr cut the count to 8-7. Lom recovered a fumble by Father Lumpkin and ran it 60 yards into the end zone, but the score was overruled by an official who claimed the whistle had blown the ball dead.

In the end, Cal was defeated and Tech crowned national champion by the narrow margin of the safety set up by Roy "Wrong Way" Riegels, who was never allowed to forget his error. "I've learned to live with it," he said a few years ago. "I've learned you can make a mistake and bounce back from it. I feel fortunate to have played football and have had the experience of playing in the Rose Bowl. I'm not bitter."

That game was the highlight of the coaching career of Bill Alexander, who spent 44 years at Georgia Tech as student, player, teacher, coach and athletic director. Hard on the outside, soft inside, "The Old Man" won 131 games in a quarter-century as head coach of the Engineers.

In 1929 another classic coach, Bernie Bierman, rose to the top. That season Notre Dame, Purdue and Tulane all were undefeated and untied. Tulane tallied 279 points, almost 100 more than either Purdue or Notre Dame. Billy "The Blond Blizzard" Blinker ran wild as Bierman's team trimmed such touted powers as Georgia, Georgia Tech, LSU and Texas A&M. The next year the Green Wave lost only to Northwestern and the following season only to USC.

Purdue, coached by Jimmy Phelan, won its first Big Ten title in 1929. Pest Welsh and Glen Harmason were the stars as the Boilermakers beat Michigan, Chicago, Wisconsin and Iowa among major rivals.

In 1928, Rockne struggled through a 5-4-1 season, the only one in which his Notre Dame teams lost more than 2 games. Their last victory, the one that assured them of at least a winning season, came against Army at Yankee Stadium.

Before the game Rockne told his team that on his deathbed the great George Gipp had told him, "Sometime, Rock, when the team is up against it, when things are wrong and the breaks are beating the boys, ask them to win one for the Gipper."

"This is that game," Rockne roared.

An inspired Irish team roared from behind to upset the Cadets, 12-6. Scoring the decisive touchdown in the end zone, Jack Chevigny hurled the ball down and hollered, "That's one for the Gipper."

It was the second time Rockne used the speech. It worked against Indiana in 1921, too.

Rockne could move men. His team bounced back in 1929, although they played all their games on the road with their new stadium under construction. They won them all, but were not as dominant as other teams at the top, winning 3 by 1 touchdown and 1 by 1 point. However they were improving. By 1930, when they put together a second straight perfect record, only 1 team came within 1 touchdown of them—they clearly were the class of the country.

Wallace Wade had another Alabama powerhouse with a perfect record put together by Sugar Cain, Fred Sington, Frank Howard and others, but the Crimson Tide's opposition could not be compared to that of the Irish. Notre Dame, led by Frank Carideo, "Jumpin' Joe" Savoldi, Moon Mullins, Marty Brill, Marchy Schwartz and many other magnificent athletes trounced most rivals in an intense intersectional schedule that included SMU, USC and Pitt.

The toughest tests came from Northwestern and Army. Northwestern held Notre Dame scoreless for 53 minutes before Carideo's punts pinned the Wildcats deep in their territory and set up 2 late Irish scores for a 14-0 victory.

Schwartz's spectacular run saved a 7-6 victory over Army. These were the only games Northwestern and Army lost all season.

The 1930 team is considered Rockne's top team. With it, he dedicated the spectacular stadium his success had created with another national championship, which, as it turned out, was his last. Headed for Hollywood to serve as technical expert on a football film, boosting the sport he had popularized, his plane crashed in a cornfield and he was killed. A great era had ended.

6

Coast-to-Coast Champps

THE 1930s WERE depression days, but not in college football. Rockne was gone but left behind a legacy of increased interest in his sport, and its importance spread coast to coast as championship contenders arose in every sector of the country.

Competition was so intense that in 1931 not a single top team was able to get through the schedule undefeated and untied. The national title went to the only undefeated team, Tennessee, which was tied by Kentucky, 6–6, in its next-to-last game.

Bob Neyland, the son of a lawyer, was born in Texas and attended Texas A&M before gaining an appointment to the Military Academy. An end on Army's undefeated teams of 1914 and 1915, he also was the school heavyweight boxing champion and a good enough baseball pitcher to get bonus bids from John McGraw of the Giants and Connie Mack of the A's.

Neyland favored football. An expert engineering student who eventually completed his studies at MIT, a man with a marvelous mind who rose to the rank of brigadier general in the service, he returned to West Point as an aide to then-superintendent Douglas MacArthur. General Neyland put his mathematical, tactical talents to use as an assistant coach at the Academy and left the service to take over at Tennessee in

1926. He taught the sport so well that at one time 100 of his former players were coaching in colleges.

College coaches at that time used many offenses, but Neyland was one of those who made the single wing the dominant formation. This featured a triple-threat tailback, usually, with a blocking quarterback and pulling guards, who left the line to lead the interference for the runners. Neyland was more interested in speed than size in his players. His team practiced precision. But he often put his top players on defense and stressed this phase of football.

Neyland pinpointed the kicking game as the key to success, often punting on third down, preferring to pin opponents in their territory and putting the pressure on them to turn the ball over to his teams in good field position. He said, "The team that makes the fewer mistakes wins. The opportunistic team wins." Neyland's Tennessee teams won. They won 173 games in his 21 years there and his .859 winning percentage is the fifth finest in football history.

Neyland coached 8 unbeaten teams. He put together a 33-game winning streak. At one point his teams lost only 1 game in 7 seasons. They shut out 42 of 62 foes in that stretch. His teams held foes to an average of less than 6 points a game in his career. His 1928 team lost the national title in a scoreless tie with Kentucky. His 1931 team laid claim to the crown despite a 6-6 tie with Kentucky. But Kentucky never defeated a Neyland team.

Neyland's 1931 team was one of his greatest, surrendering only 15 points all season. It awed Alabama, 25-0, vanquished Vanderbilt, 21-7, and nodded NYU, 13-0. It nosed out North Carolina, 7-0. The Volunteers had a clever quarterback, Bobby Dodd, who became an outstanding coach; superb runners in Gene McEvery and Beattie Feathers and a great guard in Herman Hickman.

One of the few big men to star for Neyland, Hickman was a 230-pound strong man who could run faster than most backs. He made his reputation in New York when Chick Meehan's NYU team ran 4 straight goal-line plunges at "The Fat Man" and got thrown back 10 yards. A wise and witty gentleman, he grew to more than 300 pounds in later life, wrote poetry and became coach at Yale.

After a 13-7 upset loss to St. Mary's in its opener, Howard Jones' USC team captured 10 straight games. Its 21-12 upset of Bernie Bierman's undefeated Tulane team in the Rose Bowl cleared the way for Tennessee to claim the national title. Ernie Pinckert caught a Tulane runner from behind after a 59-yard run to deprive the southerners of one score, then ran 23 and 30 yards for scores himself to highlight the 1932 New Year's Day contest.

However, USC's most dramatic victory of the season had come in the ending of the Notre Dame winning streak, which had been stretched to 25 games by new coach Hunk Anderson. This series has been one of the most spectacular in sports and was as good in years gone by as it is in these years.

The first meeting, in 1926, lured almost 75,000 fans to the Los Angeles Coliseum, and tiny Art Parisien, troubled by a heart ailment, came off the bench to beat USC, 13-12, with passes in the last minute. In 1927, USC invaded the Midwest for the first time, but lost in Chicago, 7-6. The next year, at home, the Trojans handed Rockne the last loss of his career. In 1929 a record crowd of 123,000 jammed Soldier Field to see the Irish prevail, 13-12, despite a 95-yard kickoff return by Racehorse Russell Sanders.

In 1930 Rockne coached from a wheelchair because of phlebitis, the illness that later struck President Nixon. He told his team in Los Angeles that it was so obvious from their poor practice sessions that he was the only one who wanted to win, he was going to the Mayo Clinic in Rochester instead of staying for the game. Then he secreted himself high atop the arena to watch Anderson drive the squad through as spirited a practice as the Irish ever had. After a team spokesman visited him to beg him to stay, the shrewd Rockne coached a 27-0 romp.

It was not so easy in 1931. The Irish ran at will through the Trojans to lead, 14-0, going into the final quarter, when USC reversed the course of the contest. Gus Shaver spearheaded a drive to one score, but when Johnny Baker's conversion kick was blocked by Joe Kurth, the capacity crowd in the Coliseum groaned. However, on USC's next series, quarterbacks Orv Mohler and Gus Shaver, playing in the backfield together, mounted another march to a second touchdown. Baker made this kick to put the score at 14-13.

With 3 minutes left, Shaver passed from his goal line 60 yards to Ray Sparling, who made a diving catch on the 40. Mohler then moved towering tackle Bob Hall to end to fool the Irish and passed to him at the 18. Three downs took the ball to the 13. On fourth down, in the final minute, Baker booted the field goal from the 23 that won it, 16-14, and sent the fans into a frenzy.

Moving on this momentum, USC stormed through the 1932 season undefeated and untied in 10 games to claim the national crown. Led by backs Mohler and Cotton Warburton and great guards Aaron Rosenberg and Ernie Smith, the Trojans trimmed Notre Dame, 13-0, and went on to wallop undefeated Pitt, 35-0, in the Rose Bowl.

For Jones, who previously coached national championship clubs at Yale and Iowa, this made him the only man ever to capture the title at 3 different schools. The Yale graduate, who also coached at Syracuse, Ohio State and Duke, is in the top 12 all-time coaches, with 194 victories in 29 years. The original absent-minded professor, who forgot appointments even with members of his own family, kept losing things and lost his own way home once, his mind always was filled with football. He improved on the innovations of others and said, "Take care of the fundamentals and the rest will take care of itself."

A tie with Vanderbilt aborted the Tennessee bid to repeat as titleholder in 1932. However, Harry Kipke's Michigan team, led by Harry Newman, won 8 straight over some of the top teams in the country and could claim a piece of the title.

Andy Kerr's unbeaten, untied, unscored-on and "uninvited" Colgate club, which routed rivals, 264–0, could claim a share as well. Controversy arose when it was passed over in favor of Pitt for the Rose Bowl berth. A protégé of Pop Warner, Kerr, who never played football himself, taught a razzle-dazzle game which produced 147 victories in 26 seasons at four schools.

The collegiate crown returned to the Ivies in 1933 as Princeton put together the only perfect record in the country. Fritz Crisler's Tigers blanked their first 7 foes, then surrendered 8 points in putting away their final 2 foes. Lineman Dan Hinman was the top player, but most of the starters were sophomores who wound up losing only 1 game in 3 seasons. Yale, led by Larry Kelley and Clint Frank, the second and third winners of the Heisman Trophy, stalled the Tigers in 1934, 7–0, but Princeton bounced back perfect in 1935.

Princeton handed Columbia its only defeat in 1933, 20–0. Still, Lou Little's Lions were ridiculed when picked to play in the Rose Bowl against Stanford. Little, a good coach with bad teams most of his coaching career, invented a trick play he called KF-79. He tried it early in the game, but it failed. He tried it again shortly before halftime. Quarterback Cliff

Montgomery took the center's snap, spun around, slipped the ball to Al Barabas, faked a handoff to another runner and pretended to keep the pigskin himself. While the defense pursued Montgomery, Barabas slipped around the left side unseen and untouched to score. The play lives on as a legend.

Michigan scraped through 7 victories on its durable defense, but a scoreless tie with Minnesota spoiled its record. Minnesota handed powerful Pitt its only loss, 7–3. Bernie Bierman's conservative club at Minnesota was unbeaten but had no less than 4 ties to go with 4 victories. It had the curious season scoring totals of 64–32.

Army would have been an unbeaten contender for the crown if it had not slipped in its finale with Notre Dame, 13–12.

The laurels returned to the South and Alabama in 1934, although Minnesota also put together a perfect campaign. Frank Thomas from Notre Dame, who is in the top ten all-time coaches with a .795 winning percentage over 19 seasons, was at Alabama 15 seasons and started the school's days of bowl-game glory, winning 5 of 6 postseason classics. He never had a better team than his 1934 Alabama team, which was led by a super passing combination—quarterback Dixie Howell to end Don Hutson. Alabama topped Tennessee by a touchdown and knocked over 9 other foes, including undefeated Stanford in the Rose Bowl. The tall, slender, swift Hutson caught 6 passes for 2 touchdowns and 165 yards in the 29–13 rout of Stanford, which cemented Alabama's bid for the college crown.

Minnesota could claim the crown, too. Bierman's boys mauled mighty Michigan, 34–0, and handed Pitt its only loss of the season, 13–7. This was a grueling ground duel decided in the final minutes of the final period when Pug Lund passed for the winning touchdown.

Generally, Bierman passed up the pass. His 1935 club

captured a clear-cut crown in 1935 when it ground out a second straight 8-0-0 record that made him a rare man who has won 2 national titles at two different schools. This team trounced his old Tulane team, 20-0. It handed Nebraska its lone loss of the year, 12-7, as George Roscoe ran spectacularly and powerfully to both touchdowns. Princeton also had a perfect record, but did not defeat teams of the quality of Minnesota's foes.

Bierman built an awesome line led by Bill Bevan, Butch Larson and Ed Widseth. He favored smart players, such as back Bud Wilkinson.

In retirement now, he recently told this writer, "A good running game behind good blocking is the smartest game. I pushed my players to perfect a fundamental game. Passing is a gambler's game, played by fools. I could take a team today, teach it to take the ball away from the other team on defense, control the ball on offense and beat the best of them with their new-fangled, fancy aerial attacks."

Bierman was another "absent-minded professor," so wrapped up in his profession that he once walked home from the stadium after a game, forgetting his car parked in the lot. He claimed at least a share of 5 national titles with 5 un-defeated teams in a 26-year coaching career. He used sarcasm on his players, but he never cursed or raised his voice and never gave a pep-talk. He made machines of his men but earned their respect, if not their affection. "Years later they expressed gratidude for what I had given them," he noted recently.

Two Southwest Conference clubs contended for the crown until season's end when Matty Bell's SMU team, led by Bobby Wilson, beat Dutch Meyer's TCU team, led by Slingin' Sammy Baugh, 20-14, but then bowed to Stanford in the Rose Bowl, 7-0.

The Southwest Conference classic was one of the most

memorable ever. It was the first from that sector broadcast on radio nationally and covered by the greats of sports writing. Both teams brought perfect records to the Fort Worth event.

Decoying short, skinny Wilson, SMU marched to a 14-0 lead. Baugh's "bullets" seemed to be thrown too hard to be caught as receivers dropped several perfect passes in the open. But Baugh pushed back SMU with one of his booming punts, and a poor punt by SMU paved the way for a short drive to a TCU score. At halftime, Bell told his team, "You have thirty minutes to play and a lifetime to think about it." In the second half, Baugh started to hit on his throws and passed his team to a tie, 14-14.

Jackrabbit Smith, a sub, went in, ran his SMU team into TCU territory, then on fourth down at the 37, called for a fake punt. Bob Finley faked the punt, faded back and threw a wobbler as far as he could, to where Wilson leaped and caught it as he tumbled over the goal line under a host of defenders.

Baugh popularized passing but was beaten by his receivers and rivals that day. SMU in turn was beaten by the "Vow Boys" of Stanford, a bunch led by Bobby Grayson and Bob Reynolds, who had sworn never to lose to USS, and never did, but had lost two straight Rose Bowl games before stunning SMU.

Another classic contest of that campaign frustrated Ohio State. It met Notre Dame in a duel of unbeatens before 80,000 fans in Columbus. Some said Ohio State had one of the top teams of all time. And when Frank Boucher took a lateral 65 yards to score one touchdown and led a long drive to another to give the Buckeyes a 13-0 lead, they looked like the best.

Borrowing a line from Rockne, Elmer Layden, now the Notre Dame coach, wondered aloud at intermission, "Maybe we should play your press clippings, boys." He inspired them with the insult of starting his second string the second half.

The big Buckeye line held the Irish in check in the third quarter. It was not until Andy Pilney sped 47 yards with a punt on the last play before the fourth period that the Irish started to roll.

Pilney passed from the 13 to Frank Gaul at the 1, then sent Steve Miller over to make it 13-6. But Ken Stilley missed the conversion kick. Two minutes later, the Irish got the ball back and Pilney completed 3 straight passes to reach the Ohio 1 again, but Miller fumbled the ball away and all seemed lost.

Notre Dame got the ball way back on its 22. Pilney completed 3 more passes and caught one. The coach's brother, Mike Layden, caught the one that counted to make it 13-12. But Wally Fromhart missed this conversion kick. Now what hope was left?

With the fans in a frenzy, the Irish tackled so fiercely that Beltz of the Bucks fumbled the ball away at midfield and Notre Dame had one last chance with the clock ticking away the time. Pilney faded to pass, was trapped, tore free and took off on a broken-field run that brought the ball to the 19. Screaming supporters of the Irish hushed as he lay hurt after the tackle and had to be carried off the field on a stretcher.

A back named Bill Shakespeare went in with seconds left. He passed incomplete as Beltz almost intercepted. There was time left for only one or two more plays. Shakespeare threw a prayer into the left corner where Wayne Milner, who had sneaked behind Beltz, grabbed it. Bedlam erupted in the arena. Notre Dame had won, 18-13.

The Irish had so little left they lost their next 2 games, but they had bounced the Buckeyes out of the championship chase with one of the most incredible comebacks ever in a game that has been voted the best in college football annals. Shakespeare, a super runner and passer, finished second to Jay Berwanger in the voting for the first Heisman Trophy.

The Associated Press poll appeared for the first time the following season and at the end declared Minnesota the national champion, but not all selectors agreed, choosing others in a season in which no team had a perfect record. Northwestern appears to have deserved the throne. Northwestern and Minnesota each had 7-1-0 marks. When they met Northwestern won, 6-0. Northwestern lost only to Notre Dame. Bierman feels he can claim three consecutive crowns, but the loss of a defensive duel in the mud stymied him here. Pappy Waldorf's Wildcats were not nearly as dominant but won the big one.

Alabama could claim a piece of the title, but its record was spoiled by a scoreless tie with Tennessee.

Pitt's perfect record was marred by a scoreless tie with Fordham in 1937, but in another year in which no major power was perfect Pitt prevailed. Curiously this was the third straight season Fordham, with its "seven blocks of granite" up front, led by pivot Alex Wojchichowicz and a guard by the name of Vince Lombardi, had held Pitt to a scoreless tie. Coach Jim Crowley's Rams held foes to 1 touchdown in 1936, but this brought them a 7-6 loss to NYU. They allowed only 2 touchdowns in 1937 and did not lose, but Pitt beat better teams.

Scottish-born Jock Sutherland was a "ringer" for Bernie Bierman. He was a gentler man, but demanded discipline and taught an equally powerful single-wing formation attack that relied on running, not passing, and he never gave pep-talks. When his team played well, he told them, "Well, that's what wins football games." He considered that a compliment. He coached 20 years at Lafayette and Pitt and his winning percentage of .812 is among the top ten in history. He never married. "It would distract me from my favorite sport," he said, smiling a little.

Although he had many claimants to the national title, his 1937 Pitt team seems to have been his best. It won the AP poll and most awards. It was led by the "dream backfield" of Marshall Goldberg, Chick Chickerneo, Dick Cassiano, Curly Stebbins and Frank Patrick. The only team to top the Panthers the previous season, Duquesne, was stopped, 6-0, as the great Biggie Goldberg sped 77 yards for the only score. Nebraska was beaten, 13-7. Notre Dame was beaten, 21-6.

Two West Coast clubs claimed pieces of the title. Buck Shaw's Santa Clara club surrendered only one touchdown in winning nine in a row, but beat only one top team until topping LSU, 6-0, in the Sugar Bowl in New Orleans. Now new bowl games were being held to help settle disputed national titles. Stub Allison's California club won 10 games, dealing Alabama its only loss of the season, 13-0, in the Rose Bowl, but a scoreless tie with Washington spoiled the California streak.

Carnegie Tech ended Pitt's string of 21 straight games without a loss in 1938, and that was the last year for Sutherland there. His school's authorities decided to deemphasize football. A similar situation sent Carnegie Tech from the ranks of the pigskin powers shortly thereafter. Others which went the same way were Villanova, undefeated in 1938, and Georgetown, undefeated in 1938 and 1939. And Chicago gave up the sport in 1939.

The main claimants to the 1938 college crown were Tennessee and Texas Christian, each 11-0-0. The AP picked TCU, but more selectors chose Tennessee, which merited a slim edge. Its points performance was superior at 293-16 to 269-60.

This may have been General Neyland's greatest team. The Vols were led by a brilliant back, George "Bad News" Cafego, and a lot of lethal linemen, including end Bowden Wyatt, tackle Marshall Shires and guard Bob Suffridge, the latter small but so quick and strong a tackler and blocker he has since been named an all-time All-Star.

Tennessee had a couple of close calls, clipping Auburn, 7-0 and LSU, 14-0, but climaxed its campaign with a 17-0 defeat of previously undefeated Oklahoma in the Orange Bowl in Miami. Tennessee shut out its last 5 foes. In fact, it allowed only 6 touchdowns in winning 30 straight regular-season games from 1938 through 1940.

The master of defense, Duke's Wallace Wade almost pulled off a modern miracle and a national title in 1938 when he led his team through an undefeated, untied and unscored-on regular season until cut down in the last minute of the last game, the New Year's Day, 1939, Rose Bowl classic.

Led by great runner George McAfee, super punter Eric Tipton and a determined line, Duke led, 3-0, on Tony Ruffa's field goal until Howard Jones gambled on a fourth-string quarterback, who was not a top player but was his best passer. Doyle Nave completed 8 straight passes, the last one to Al Krueger in the end zone in the gathering gloom to bring USC a dramatic 7-3 triumph in one of the great games.

Wade who had wonderful teams at Alabama and Duke in winning 171 games in 24 years, once said, "The best you do is not good enough unless it does the job." After the Rose Bowl, he sat sadly in a dispirited dressing room and said, "Our best just wasn't good enough."

USC lost 2 games that season, but dealt California and Notre Dame, as well as Duke, their only defeats. The only other undefeated team at the top was TCU with its tiny star, Davey O'Brien, the successor to Slingin' Sammy Baugh as the Southwest's top tosser. Dutch Meyer's team threw 229 passes and lost only 7 on interceptions. Most of the passes were by the 5-6, 150-pound O'Brien. He set new college records by completing 55 percent of his passes for almost 1,500 yards. His team won most of its starts easily until losing to Carnegie Tech, 15–7, in the Cotton Bowl in Dallas.

The Southwest did capture a clear-cut national title the next season as Texas A&M won the AP and most other awards. Jarrin' John Kimbrough, a big fullback, operated effectively behind a strong line led by Joe Boyd and Marshall Robnett. Coach Homer Norton's team won all 11 of its starts, though narrowly escaping with a 14–13 victory over previously undefeated Tulane in the Sugar Bowl.

The Rose Bowl was Tennessee's undoing. That team was undefeated, untied and unscored on after 10 games. Unbeaten, but twice-tied USC, for the second straight season spoiled a foe's scoreless streak, with a 14–0 victory. This ended the Vols' 24-game winning streak and 30-game unbeaten streak.

The near-miss unscored-on runs of Duke and Tennessee have not been matched since, for college football entered an era of emphasis on offense. Carl Shavely's Cornell club, led by Brud Holland and Nick Draaos upset Ohio State and had a perfect record in 1939, but that was the last time an Ivy League team was considered a claimant for the national title. Eastern powers had started to deemphasize football, and schools from other sectors had shot to the top.

7

The War Years

THE LITTLE LEFT-HANDER, Frankie Albert, crouched directly behind the center, who handed the ball to him. Albert spun, handing off to a runner angling into the line, faking a hand-off, hiding the ball, then drifting back to pass downfield to a receiver while most of the opposing team was tackling the supposed ballcarrier.

This was the T-formation offense as devised by Clark Shaughnessy, who helped George Halas put it into pro football with the Chicago Bears in 1939. The Bears captured the championship playoff from the Washington Redskins that year by the astonishing score of 73-0. He then took it to Stanford in 1940, which captured the college crown with it.

It was not entirely new. Amos Alonzo Stagg had used it in the late 1890s and early 1900s. When forward passing was permitted, he experimented with flanker backs—potential receivers split farther outside the offensive line than ends normally played. Pop Warner, Frank Cavanaugh and Knute Rockne used it, using a man in motion to distract the defense.

However, it had drifted into disuse as the single-wing offense became the dominant offense of the sport through the 1920s and 1930s. In this, the tailback stood deep in the backfield and received the snap from center to start plays in motion. These were primarily power, running plays, although he was safely far enough from defenders to set for passes, too.

Admitting he had adapted an ancient attack while assisting at the University of Chicago and studying with Halas of the Bears, Shaughnessy took a chance with it when he went to Stanford. Veterans figured him for a fool. Even Warner wondered if the system wasn't washed up. "If Stanford wins a single game with that crazy formation, you can throw all the football I ever knew into the Pacific Ocean," he snorted.

Stanford, which had won only a single game the year before, won 10 games with the new formation—including the Rose Bowl game—merited the national title and reshaped the sport. Although diehards such as Crisler at Michigan, Bierman at Minnesota and Neyland at Tennessee were still taking titles with the single wing years later, the vast majority of the coaches in the country had converted to the "T" within ten years.

This was an offense of speed and deception. As defenses have adjusted to it, it has altered to become the "Split T," the "Wishbone," the "I" the "Veer," and other such variations. Defenses have altered to meet the new offenses, pulling men out of the forward wall to increase the number of linebackers and defensive backs, devising "zone" pass defenses and so forth. But Shaughnessy's "T" is the base on which every modern offense is built.

He coached college ball 31 years and won 149 games. And he coached pro titlists, too. However, he never had as great a year as he had in 1940 at Stanford. He had ideal men to become the backs in his new formation—small but slick and daring Albert at quarterback, powerful Norm Standlee at fullback, swift Hugh Gallarneau and Pete Kmetovic at halfbacks. And he had quick, agile linemen, led by Chuck Taylor and Bruno Banducci.

Albert insists Shaughnessy deserves all the credit. "A lesser man would have been afraid to try something so radical," he says. "We ourselves were skeptical. But he sold us on it. After all, we'd been so bad the year before, we felt we had little to lose. As it wound up, all we did was win. Luck plays a part. We had talent we were wasting, which was just right for this new system. But the coach still had to teach it to us, and fast."

Stanford barely got by Santa Clara, 7-6, in the early season and had several other close calls as the season wore on, but they beat Southern Cal by 2 touchdowns and UCLA and Cal by 1 each, and by the time they got to the Rose Bowl they were ready to prove they were the best. Nebraska had been beaten by Minnesota, 13-7, in their opener but had remained unbeaten since then and represented a stiff test.

Nebraska marched 79 yards to lead, 7-0. Albert turned the "T" loose, sending Kmetovic off to 2 long runs and Gallarneau for an 11-yarder through confused defenders to tie. Nebraska recovered a fumble and swept in to regain the lead at 13-7. But Albert slipped back into the blocking pocket and passed to Gallarneau for 40 yards and another score. With Albert's second of 3 conversions, Stanford led at halftime, 14-13.

In the second half, Kmetovic returned a punt 61 yards to seal the victory, 21-13, and history had been made. The AP and others already had named Minnesota national titleholder, but the Helms Hall of Fame board and others who waited for results of the bowl games recognized Stanford as the king.

Minnesota had another mighty team, led by Bruce Smith, and overcame eight straight foes, but barely got by Northwestern and Michigan by a point each. That was the only loss for Michigan, led by Tom Harmon and Al Wistert. Harmon's pass put Michigan in front, 6-0, but the conversion kick was missed. Smith's 80-yard scoring run and a successful conversion won it for Minnesota, 7-6.

Harmon, one of the great broken-field runners of all time, won the Heisman Trophy that year, and Smith, an outstanding all-around performer, took it the next year.

In his second season as coach, Frank Leahy brought Boston College to a perfect record, climaxed by a 19-13 upset of Tennessee in the Sugar Bowl. That was the only loss for Neyland's Tennessee team. Boston College had great athletes in Charley O'Rourke, Mike Holovak, Gene Goodreault, Chet Gladchuk and Fred Naumetz. Tennessee was led by Bob Suffridge, Marshall Shires, Johnny Butler and Bobby Foxx.

Homer Norton's Texas A&M team, led by John Kimbrough, had their season spoiled by a 7-0 loss to Texas, but bounced back to nip Fordham in the Cotton Bowl, 13-12.

There was no disputing Minnesota's right to the title in 1941 as Bierman's bruisers, led by Smith and tackle Dick Wildung, comprised the only team to put together a perfect record. The Golden Gophers nipped Northwestern by a point and Michigan and Washington by a touchdown each in winning 8 straight.

Bierman went off to World War II as a marine officer, and when he returned the game and the boys who played it had changed. He coached 6 more seasons, but they hung him in effigy before he retired. He had won or shared 7 national titles. Only Rockne shared in more. "They thought I was an old man so I guessed it was time to go," he recalled regretfully when we talked to him, still stern and ramrod straight in retirement.

Leahy's first Notre Dame team went undefeated, but won one game by only a single point, another by 2 and was held to a scoreless tie by Army. Wallace Wade had one of his greatest Duke teams, which outscored rivals, 311-41, and went undefeated in the regular season but was upset, 20-14, by Oregon State in a Rose Bowl game. This was played at Duke's

Durham campus after being switched from the West Coast following the Japanese air attack on Pearl Harbor, December 7, and the start of the war.

Maybe it was wartime madness, but for a while in 1941 a small school seemed so strong it threatened to contend for all laurels. This was Plainfield Teachers College, whose scores as it trounced team after team, and whose star, a Chinese halfback named John Chung, started to attract attention on the sports pages of the major newspapers. Sadly, there was no such school or star.

Some Wall Street brokers, observing the scores of little-known colleges in Sunday's editions, decided to invent a team, foes, games and scores. Posing as "stringers," they called the major dailies and wire services and reported dreamed-up contests.

What started as a prank progressed to the point that as Plainfield's triumphs mounted, the funsters rented a telephone to answer requests for information. They sent out publicity releases featuring their fictional star. Feature stories spread this imaginary school's success story nationwide. Then a reporter sent to do a story at the school couldn't find the college and the hoax was revealed and ended—to the embarrassment of some of the biggest newspapers in the country.

The highest-scoring team in 1941 was Texas, which was real and played real people. The Longhorns totalled 338 points behind Jackrabbit Crain, Pete Layden and Mel Kutner, but they were tied by Baylor and beaten by TCU. Wally Butts' Georgia Bulldogs were almost as explosive and trounced TCU in the Orange Bowl, but they were tied by Mississippi and beaten by Alabama.

Georgia reached the top in 1942. There was not an unbeaten team in the country, but the Bulldogs' 11 victories in 12 starts seems to have been the best record. The AP already had picked Ohio State, but most selectors turned to Georgia after the Bulldogs stopped UCLA in the Rose Bowl, 9-0. Heisman Trophy winner Frank Sinkwich totalled 2,200 yards on offense, the record at that time. Sinkwich scored the only touchdown in the bowl battle, but he was in and out of the game with sore ankles. A sensational sophomore, Charlie Trippi, filled in flawlessly.

Georgia lost only to Auburn and bounced back in the last game of the regular season to knock Georgia Tech from the ranks of the unbeaten. Ohio State, led by Les Horvath and Bill Willis, lost only to Wisconsin. This was Paul Brown's best team, but he coached at Ohio State only 3 seasons. He went away to war and returned to pro prominence.

For most of the season Boston College was touted as the top team with super players in Holovak, Don Currivan, Gil Bouley, Rocco Canale and Fred Naumetz. And it was undefeated until its traditional finale with weak Holy Cross. It underestimated the Crusaders, who were inspired and crushed the Eagles, 55-12, in one of the most astonishing reversals of form in football annals. The disappointed losers cancelled the party they had planned at the Coconut Grove night club in Boston. There was a fire that night in the night club and more than 400 persons died.

Notre Dame returned to the top in 1943, the first of the national titles Leahy could claim before he concluded a classic coaching career.

Leahy played on Rockne's last three teams at Notre Dame. He was not a great player, but a smart one and dedicated. Before Rockne died he recommended Leahy for the assistant's job at Georgetown, which commenced Leahy's coaching career. Later he assisted at Michigan State and at Fordham, where he tutored, among others, Vince Lombardi. Leahy became head man at Boston College and had 1 undefeated season in 2 years there, then moved to Notre Dame where he had 5 undefeated seasons in 11 years.

His first title team was tremendous. It was led by quarterback Angelo Bertelli, a skilled passer and winner of the Heisman Trophy, and included such runners as Creighton Miller and Julie Rykovich and such linemen as Pat Filley and Jim White. It slaughtered such formidable foes as Georgia Tech by 55–13; Wisconsin, by 50–0; Illinois, by 47–0; Pitt, by 41–0; Michigan, by 35–12; Navy, by 33–6, and Army, by 26–0. Wisconsin and Navy lost only to Notre Dame. Bertelli was called into the service after the sixth game, and a splendid sophomore, Johnny Lujack, handled the romp over Army.

Lujack also had to lead the Irish in their final 2 games, which were stiff tests against service teams stocked with college stars. Leahy's lads got by Iowa Pre-Flight, 14–13, but were beaten by Great Lakes 19–14, on a scoring pass from former Duke star Steve Lach with 19 seconds left.

At Great Lakes Naval Training Station, Bertelli listened to the bitter end. He recalls, "I was in tears. Then someone handed me a telegram. I opened it and read that I'd won the Heisman Trophy. For half a season. If ever a man had mixed emotions, it was me."

Since the defeat had come at the hands of a service powerhouse, Notre Dame nevertheless was the first unanimously-named national champion among all major selectors. However, there was one team with a perfect record that season, Purdue, and the Boilermakers did beat Great Lakes, 23–13. Maybe the Boilermakers really rated the title, which they never have won. Coach Elmer Burnham's team won nine in a row with such stars as Babe Dimancheff, Bump Elliott, Tony Butkovich, Dick Barwegan and Alex Agase.

Both Notre Dame and Purdue benefitted from standouts shifted from other schools into their university service training programs. Also, several schools such as Alabama, Tennessee, Auburn, Mississippi and others cancelled their schedules because of the war.

By 1944, few could compete with the Army team. The West Point program was packed with outstanding athletes, many of them transfers from other colleges. The Naval Academy enjoyed equal benefits, but its teams were not as successful. Credit must be given Cadet coach Red Blaik, who built Army's powerhouses. He put together 2 consecutive perfect seasons in gaining back-to-back national titles in 1944 and 1945.

Blaik, the first Cadet to face Navy in three sports, graduated from West Point and rose to the rank of colonel in the cavalry before retiring to coach at Dartmouth, then went back to the Point. At one time at Dartmouth he went 23 straight games without a defeat. Still, some feel he did not prove his immortality until he followed his first two championship teams at Army with three more undefeated claimants to the title later, after other college clubs had their strength restored.

Blaik said, "Luck doesn't win games. If you are properly prepared, you make your own luck." He was a methodical man but a keen student of his sport and a sharp strategist.

His wartime teams of Army had great athletes in Glenn Davis, Doc Blanchard, Arnold Tucker, Tex Coulter, Hank Foldberg, Barney Poole and many more. Blanchard became "Mr. Inside" and Davis "Mr. Outside" as they ran roughshod over rivals.

The 6-0, 205-pound Blanchard was the heavy-duty guy and averaged almost 6 yards a carry in his college career. The 5-9, 170-pound Davis was the breakaway runner who averaged 8 yards a carry for 4 years and twice set records by averaging 11 yards. Davis, a spectacular broken-field runner to rank with

Red Grange and Tom Harmon, won the Heisman Trophy in 1945. Blanchard won it the next year.

Davis had scoring runs of 44, 46, 50, 53, 55, 58, 60, 63 and 73 yards while scoring 20 touchdowns in 1944. Army sank the Navy, 23-7, embarrassed Notre Dame, 59-0, and routed other rivals by such scores as 46-0, 59-7, 62-7, 69-7, 76-0 and 83-0. The following year Davis had scoring runs of 41, 47, 48, 65, 70, 72, 77 and 87 yards while scoring 18 touchdowns. Army knocked off the Navy, 32-13, again embarrassed Notre Dame, 48-0, and ran up scores such as 54-0, 54-0, 55-13 and 61-0 on others.

No college clubs even belonged in the same ball park with the Cadets these years, though some had excellent seasons.

In 1944 Ohio State, with Carrol Widdoes coaching and Les Horvath and Bill Willis starring, won all 9 of its starts. Only a good Michigan team came close at 18-14.

In 1945, Alabama, with Frank Thomas coaching, and Harry Gilmer and Vaughn Mancha starring, took 10 in a row and ran up 55 points three times, 60 points and 71 points on rivals. Oklahoma A&M also was undefeated and untied that year with Jim Lookabaugh coaching and Bob Fennimore starring. Indiana was undefeated, but tied by Northwestern. Bo McMillan was the coach of the Hoosiers' greatest team, which rostered such standouts as George Taliaferro, Pete Pihos, Bob Ravensberg, Ted Kluszewski, John Goldsberry, Howard Brown and John Cannady.

However, Army was a unanimous choice for the national title in both 1944 and 1945. It was not until 1946 after the war had ended that the Cadets' hold on the college crown was threatened.

Princeton v. Cornell, 1903—before players were required to wear helmets. (*Courtesy Princeton University*)

Fielding H. Yost, who coached Michigan to victory in the early years of this century. (*Courtesy University of Michigan*)

Amos Alonzo Stagg as a young coach (left) and as a veteran of more than a half century of coaching (right). (*Courtesy Yale University, Pacific College*)

John Heisman, coach for Georgia Tech, 1917. (*Courtesy Georgia Tech*)

Jim Thorpe (center) with two other stars of Carlisle's 1911 title team—Joe Guyon (left) with Pete Calac—before the start of a snowy game. (*Hall of Fame*)

Red Grange with coach Bob Zuppke during their title season at Illinois in 1923. (*Courtesy University of Illinois*)

Knute Rockne gives one of his celebrated pep talks to his Notre Dame team. (*Courtesy University of Notre Dame*)

Peter Pund, Georgia Tech, 1928. (*Courtesy Georgia Tech*)

The "Four Horsemen" of Notre Dame's 1924 season. From left to right: Don Miller, Elmer Layden, "Sleepy Jim" Crowley, Harry Stuhldreher. (*Courtesy University of Notre Dame*)

Roy "Wrong Way" Riegels was stunned to find he had run toward his own goal line after recovering a Georgia Tech fumble.
(*Pasadena Tournament of Roses Association*)

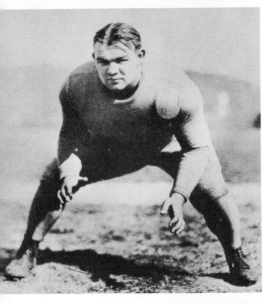

Herman, Hickman, Tennessee, 1931. (*Courtesy University of Tennessee*)

Don Hutson, Alabama, 1933. (*Courtesy University of Alabama*)

Fordham's famed "Seven Blocks of Granite" played Pitt to three straight scoreless ties in the 1930's. Front: Druze, Babartsky, Lombardi, Wojciechowicz, Pierce, Franco, Paquin. Rear: Mautte, Lock, Palan, and Gurske. (*Courtesy Fordham University*)

Leaders of West Point's World War II powerhouse: coach Red Blaik flanked by Doc Blanchard (left) and Glenn Davis (right) in 1944. (*Courtesy United States Military Academy*)

Davey O'Brien, who pitched TCU to a share of the college crown in 1938, passes against Arkansas. (*Courtesy Texas Christian University*)

Glenn Davis tears away from his Navy pursuers, 1944. (*Courtesy United States Military Academy*)

Kyle Rote of SMU just misses pass receiver Bill Wightkin of Notre Dame. (*Courtesy Southern Methodist University*)

The 1959 college king, Syracuse, in action against Texas, with David Sarette faking to Art Baker and handing off to Al Bemiller. (*Courtesy Southwest Conference*)

Coach John McKay is carried off the field by his victorious USC team. (*Courtesy University of Southern California*)

Darrell Royal, coach of the Texas team, 1969. (*Courtesy University of Texas*)

Navy's John Sai is surrounded by Texas defenders: David McWilliams (50), Tim Doerr (32), Tommy Nobis (60), and Phil Harris (25). (*Courtesy Southwest Conference*)

Ohio State's offense gets a workout in this scoring plunge in the Rose Bowl triumph of USC that wrapped up the 1968 national title. (*Courtesy Pasadena Tournament of Roses Association*)

Coach Woody Hayes calls to his Ohio players. (*Courtesy Pasadena Tournament of Roses Association*)

Nebraska's Jerry Tagge prepares to pass against LSU defense in the Orange Bowl victory concluding the championship campaign of 1970. (*Courtesy Orange Bowl Committee*)

Penn State's Heisman Trophy winner John Cappaletti concludes a scoring run on a freezing day in 1973, helping his team to another undefeated season. (*Courtesy Penn State University*)

8

Leahy's Glory Days

Doc Blanchard, as fast as he was strong, turned the right flank and fled down the right sidelines. Army's blockers had cut down Notre Dame defenders. The fullback was free as he crossed midfield, seemingly certain to snap the scoreless tie. Almost 75,000 fans stood up and started to scream on this second Saturday in November 1946.

This was about as big as a game can be. Red Blaik's Cadets had clobbered 25 consecutive foes and were well on their way to a third straight undefeated national championship season. But World War II had ended, discharged servicemen had rejoined their college clubs and Frank Leahy had returned to a Notre Dame team restored to its prewar power.

Humiliated by 59-0 and 48-0 wallopings during the war the two preceding seasons, the Irish thirsted for revenge. End zone seats were sold by scalpers for $200 apiece. Midfield locations went for twice that much. Yankee Stadium, New York, was packed for this renewal of a spectacular series, and the contest was living up to its tremendous buildup.

As big Blanchard roared down the right stripe he seemed certain to go the full 58 yards to the game's first and maybe decisive score. And then a Notre Dame player was seen angling across the field at tremendous speed to catch the Cadet star. This was before two-platoon football. The player was Johnny Lujack, Notre Dame's All-American quarterback, driving desperately at the All-American fullback.

As waves of sound washed over them from the farthest reaches of that triple-tiered arena, Lujack caught Blanchard. Lujack hit him hard; Blanchard's legs pumped and he pulled forward trying to tear free. But Lujack would not be shaken off; his arms locked around the runner. The impact seemed to send a shudder through both for a second, then Blanchard toppled over, Lujack on top of him.

The run had been aborted at 22 yards, 37 yards short of the Irish goal line. The offensive star, Lujack, never made a more memorable play than this defensive gem. The Irish braced and the struggle remained scoreless.

It was a bitter battle. Army threatened first. Red Sitko was jarred loose from the ball and Goble Bryant recovered for the Cadets on the Notre Dame 23 in the opening minutes. Blanchard was thrown for a 3-yard loss. Quarterback Arnold Tucker passed to Blanchard's spectacular All-American running mate, Glenn Davis, for 7. Blanchard blasted for 3. But then on fourth down, Blanchard, blasting again, was stopped short by big Bill Fisher and Lujack at the 14, a yard short.

Later in the period, a pass from Tucker to Blanchard covered 24 yards to the Irish 23, but the Notre Dame defense hurled Blanchard and Davis back on the following carries. Early in the second period, Lujack's passes and Gerry Cowhig's runs produced 4 straight first downs and carried Notre Dame to the Army 13. Cowhig cut across the line for 3. Gompers ground out 6 yards to the 4. But the Cadet line braced and stopped Irish runners cold on the next 2 downs to regain possession in the shadow of their own goal line.

Such great goal-line stands frustrated the offenses as the

rival coaches, lacking quality place-kickers, passed up field-goal opportunities.

Early in the second half, Lujack was passing the Irish into scoring position when his rival quarterback, Tucker, intercepted at the Cadet 10 and returned the ball 32 yards before being downed. From here, Blanchard broke free for what seemed sure to be the game-breaker before Lujack knifed him down. Neither team again mounted so serious a threat.

As the attackers wearied under assault, defenses dominated. Notre Dame took to the air in desperation, but its throws were thwarted. Four of Lujack's passes were intercepted, 3 by Tucker. In the waning moments, Army mounted one final march. Tucker took his third interception to his 43. Contained all day, Davis wriggled free for 5 yards, then took a Tucker pass for 8 more. But, on this cold, darkening day, Tucker threw and, appropriately, Lujack intercepted. The crowd was hushed.

The gun sounded to conclude a scoreless struggle. In the Notre Dame dressing room, Leahy weary and disappointed—but relieved—went to Lujack, smiled and said, "Tell me, John, how did you happen to throw so many passes to Tucker?"

Grimy, and worn down, Lujack looked up, smiled weakly and said, "He was the only man I could find open."

Leahy later observed, "When two great teams meet, defense tends to dominate." Blaik added, "A tie was a fitting end to this contest."

The tie marred the season records for both teams, but both appeared to be the best in a season in which only one team, Wally Butts' Georgia team, led by Charley Trippi and Johnny Rauch, went undefeated and untied.

No other team came closer than 3 touchdowns to the Irish, who won the AP and most other awards. Army had their hands full before downing Michigan, 20-13—and almost more than they could handle from a gallant Navy team that had lost 7 straight games but barely fell, 21-18. Blanchard and Davis ran wild. Army led, 21-6, at halftime and seemed ready to romp before 100,000 fans, including President Harry S Truman, in Philadelphia. Blanchard had run 52 yards on one play, Davis 46 on another.

Early in the second half Army marched to the Navy 32. Rather than gamble on fourth down with 2 yards to go, the Cadets punted. Davis sliced the ball out of bounds only 10 yards deep. Navy then sailed 78 yards to its second touchdown. Army got the ball back and, curiously, elected to gamble on fourth down with 1 yard to go on its own 35. Blanchard was stopped without gain, Navy took over and moved in for another tally.

Three missed conversions left the Middies short at 21-18. With time running short, they mounted a last march from their 33. They moved to the Cadets' 23 but seemed to stall there. Then on fourth down Lynn Chewning knifed free for 20 yards to the Army 3.

Ninety seconds remained and the ballpark was in bedlam. Chewning carried once, then again as time ticked away. With no more time-outs, Bill Hawkins tried a lateral to Bill Earl, but he was banged down on the 5. The gun sounded before Navy could run its fourth down. Army, the 28-point favorite, had won by 3 but had lost the national title.

In 1947 Army invaded little Baker Field to take on Columbia's lightly heralded team before 35,000 fans in New York. Blanchard and Davis were gone, but a lot of top players remained. Army led, 20-7, after 3 periods. Columbia cut this to 20-14 in the final period when end Bill Swiacki, who made amazing catches all afternoon, made the most amazing catch of his career. Diving full length, he scooped into his hands inches off the end zone ground a low throw from Gene Rossides 28 yards away.

Then, at the end, Lou Little's gallant Lions drove 72 yards, and Lou Kusserow crashed over for the tying touchdown. Ventan Yablonski's third consecutive conversion kick was perfect. Army had lost a stunner, 21–20, its 32-game un-defeated streak snapped, and it was out of the national title picture.

Two teams compiled perfect records that season, Notre Dame and Michigan. Notre Dame knocked off 9 straight, including Army by 27–7. It narrowly nosed out Northwestern, however, 26–19. Leahy's Irish, led by Lujack, Sitko and Connor, were outstanding and captured AP and other honors. However, Michigan, which may have been better, won just as many awards.

The Wolverines had taken 10 in a row. The team's last one, a 49–0 Rose Bowl rout of a USC team that had lost to Notre Dame by 31 points, came after the polls closed. This appears to have earned it the national title. This was the second straight rout of the Pacific Coast entry and the second of 6 straight victories by Big Ten teams after they entered an agreement to send a representative to the Pasadena post-season classic annually.

Liberalized substitution rules set up to ease the return of veterans to postwar teams prompted Crisler to experiment with two-platoon football, featuring separate offensive and defensive units. This altered the shape of the sport forever. Although sticking to the old-fashioned single-wing, the coach modernized his approach so that players no longer had to go both ways and could specialize.

With such players as Bob Chappius, Bump Elliott, Pete

Elliott, Len Ford, Bruce Hilkene, Len Ford and Bobby Mann, the Wolverines were overpowering, got by rugged rivals Minnesota and Illinois by a touchdown each and routed their final four foes by 145-6. Crisler, who coached 18 seasons at Princeton, Minnesota and Michigan, never had a better season. He retired after it.

A great end on past Michigan teams, Benny Oosterban, took over and retained the laurels for the Wolverines in 1948, despite the graduation of many of his stars. Wistert, the big tackle, was the only All-American on this team, but it had balance, depth and muscle. Michigan State and Illinois came within a touchdown and Ohio State came within 10 points of Michigan, but no one could knock the Wolverines from the top. Frank Howard's Clemson club was the only other team with a perfect record, and it met mostly mediocre rivals.

Army and Notre Dame each went undefeated, but each was tied once. In one of the most startling upsets of all time, Army, which had not lost a game, was tied, 21-21, by Navy, which had not won a game. This was their season finale at Philadelphia and left 102,000 fans limp. All 6 touchdowns were scored on long marches as the contest see-sawed back and forth. Army's Arnie Galiffa bootlegged the ball around end twice to put Army ahead, 21-14, in the fourth period, but Bill Hawkins battered the Cadets on a series of smashes that spearheaded a 50-yard drive, scoring on a fourth-down blast to end it all even. Inspiration makes up for much in traditional rivalries.

Notre Dame also lost a shot at the title in a tie in its last game in another great traditional series, the one with USC. The Irish were heavily favored, but the underdog Trojans were ready. Leon Hart, the enormous end, took a pass from Frank Tripucka on the USC 40 and rammed the rest of the way through the tackles of 10 Trojans, who could not get him down. USC battled back to take the lead, 14–7, near the end.

As the two teams lined up for the kickoff, Notre Dame's Bill Gay approached an official. "Mr. Referee, how much time is left?" he asked.

"Two minutes and thirty-five seconds," the referee replied.

"Thank you, sir, we have enough time," Gay said.

They did, thanks to Gay, who took the kickoff 87 yards to the Southern Cal 12. Four plays later, Red Sitko sliced over, Steve Oracko place-kicked the extra point and the contest was concluded in a stalemate, preserving another undefeated season for Notre Dame.

Another in 1949, not only undefeated, but also untied, brought the college crown back to South Bend, although Army and Oklahoma also put together perfect records.

Blaik's Cadets nipped Penn by a point, avenged themselves on Navy, 38–0, and swamped 6 other foes, including Michigan. But Notre Dame had been dropped from the Army schedule and the slate was not as strong as that of other top teams. Bud Wilkinson was building a powerhouse team in Oklahoma. The Sooners, led by Darrell Royal, Jim Owens, Dee Andros, Jim Weatherall, Wade Walker and Leon Heath took 10 straight, including LSU in a 35–0 Sugar Bowl romp. However, a narrow 1-touchdown triumph over Santa Clara reduced the Sooner reputation.

As Michigan had been the year before, Notre Dame was unanimously acclaimed king of college football in 1949. The Irish had a tremendous team topped by the massive end and fullback Leon Hart, one of only two linemen ever to win the Heisman Trophy, and such other All-Americans as Jim Martin, quarterback Bob Williams and Sitko, the veteran running star.

In its opener, Notre Dame routed Indiana, 49–6. In its ninth game, the Irish ripped USC, 32–0. In between, no one came closer than 3 touchdowns to the Irish. It was not until its tenth and last game that the Irish were threatened.

This was one of the classic contests of all time. More than 75,000 fans crammed into the Cotton Bowl in Dallas to see SMU test the Irish, but the Mustangs were without their great runner, Doak Walker, who was injured, so they seemed without hope. However, sophomore substitute Kyle Rote, found fame this day.

Bill Wightkin caught a ball behind Rote and ran into the end zone to put the Irish in front early. John Champion passed the ball to Johnny Milam for 78 yards to put the Mustangs in close, but the Irish took over after Rote's fourth-down drive was stopped 6 inches short of the goal line. The Irish marched the length of the field and Williams' pass bounced off defenders' hands into Ernie Zalejski's hands and it was 13-0 at intermission.

In the second half, Rote ran wild. Running, passing or threatening a pass on almost every play, he pushed his side 62 yards to its first score. An intercepted pass from Rote put the Irish on the Mustang 22 and they stormed over to make it 20-7. Rote promptly passed to Champion for 68 yards to the 1, then dove over and it was 20-14. After the kickoff, a penalty put the Irish in a hole. Champion fielded a punt at midfield and put it on the 14. Rote rolled right twice to score and it was 20-20, but Billy Sullivan's place-kick was blocked.

This was a Notre Dame team of championship caliber and it refused to cave in as bedlam broke out in the old bowl. Behind brutal blocking, Irish runners drove 56 yards over enemy ground to a 27-20 lead with Bill Barrett bolting across from the 6 in the tenth play of the march.

In the last 6 minutes, Rote ran and passed SMU deep into Notre Dame territory. Fred Benners' fourth-down pass took the ball 23 yards to the Irish 5. But big Jerry Groom led a defensive charge that blocked two line plunges, then picked off Rote's jump pass on his 2-yard-line. The Mustangs' upset dreams died dramatically; the vast turnout of Texans sat back down sadly.

Afterwards Leahy said, "This Notre Dame team was the greatest I ever coached."

He coached some great ones and would coach one more which would go undefeated to the national title in his last year four years later. He coached one unbeaten team in two years at Boston College and six in 13 years at Notre Dame and shared in eight national titles. He lost only 13 games in 13 seasons at Notre Dame, a record surpassed only by Rockne, who lost 12 games in 13 years. Leahy's career percentage of .864, on a 107-13-9 record, is second in coaching history only to Rockne's .881, on a 105-12-5 mark. There are those who say there were many more great teams in Leahy's day, that the competition was more intense and no one ever was better.

A gloomy guy, he used to say he didn't see how he could win, but he almost always did. Like the early coaches, Leahy was a moralistic man. He preached a player's devotion to God, country and his teammates. He admittedly neglected his own family and everything else in his life in favor of football. In his last days, he told this writer, "I pressed for perfection. I wanted my young men to be the best and I wanted always to win. I set almost impossible goals for myself, such as going undefeated ten years in a row, yet I came close to them. To this end, I used to get terribly worked up. I was very, very nervous. I could never eat on game days. I seldom slept as the game approached and seldom the night after a game. I shut myself off from most pleasures in life so I could pursue my passion."

He was not beloved by his boys. He drove them too hard. He gave them too many impassioned pep talks, sermonized too often. He imitated his idol, Rockne, and was a superb story-teller. But there was an air of theatricality about him that turned off some young men, who were becoming increasingly sophisticated in a modern era. He bent the rules to give his side every advantage, which soured some. Still, he succeeded. He was feared and respected.

He said, "I demanded a great deal of my athletes, but I could not have gotten it from them if they had not been willing to give it. I believe yes, I had some subtle chemistry of personality that enabled me to communicate, to reach and inspire my lads. I raised their thresholds of pain and inspired them to sacrifice for success. Football, like life, can be likened to war. I became their leader in battles. We fight many battles in life. Even in football, to lose is to taste death. So man suffers some. What matters is to what end: to reach something frivolous and unrewarding or to bring out the best that is in you? I brought out the best in my boys because they became the best."

He retired early at 45 after the administration at Notre Dame decided to deemphasize football in order to emphasize the scholastic side of life at the university. "Without an adequate number of scholarships to recruit the top players, my dream of ten straight undefeated seasons had ended and the future appeared to be headed downhill. I quit after one more undefeated season, while I was still on top," he said. "Years later, the university realized the error of its ways. After many years in which our school's great tradition had been hurt horribly, the authorities moved to restore its great image through great football teams. By then it was too late for me to return. But I had missed coaching terribly," Leahy commented.

In his prime, he was a proud man, erect, stern, righteous, shrewd, resourceful, tough, tremendously successful. Now, past his prime and long removed from the battle, he had been thrust into the shadows, the victim of leukemia. He was in terrible pain. He had to be helped around. Yet he got around, giving speeches. Inside he had not altered.

He sighed, his hands shaking. "It is said that I am a man who has lived beyond his time, a preacher of old-fashioned virtues that no longer are popular, a coach who could not command respect today. Yet I give speeches, I see lads listening intently and I am applauded and my counsel is sought out. I'll tell you," he said, "if I were coaching today I would do no less than I did before and I would expect as much."

Twenty years after he had coached his last undefeated champion college football team, ending another great era, he died.

9

The Wilkinson Way

STRIVING FOR ITS 40th consecutive victory without defeat, Notre Dame was defeated in the second game of the 1950 season by Purdue, 28-14. However, the magnitude of that upset was diminished when the Irish were trimmed by Indiana two weeks later, and by Michigan State the next week, then tied by Iowa and topped by Southern Cal at season's end. The 4-4-1 season was to be the worst of Leahy's regime and the only one in which he would lose more than 2 games.

Seeking another undefeated national title season, Army was shocked by another lowly Navy team in the finale for the second time in 3 seasons. The Middies had lost 6 of 8 games and been beaten badly, but this is a sport of spirit in which a bad team can beat a good one on an inspired day, as Navy did on the last day of the season, 14-2.

Bob Blaik quarterbacked this Army team and was involved with virtually the entire roster in a cribbing scandal the following season, which all but finished off the Cadets as a college power, though his father continued to coach 7 more seasons. Red Blaik had put together 28-game and 32-game undefeated streaks and lost only 3 games in 7 seasons prior to the scandal.

Bob Neyland put together one of his greatest Tennessee teams in 1950, but the new decade was one in which new coaches and new teams would surge into the spotlight. Three teams fought for the top spot in 1950—Tennessee, Kentucky and Oklahoma—and in the end there was not one that escaped defeat. Tennessee was shocked in its second start by a 7-0 loss to Mississippi State. It did not lose again and beat top teams in Alabama, 14-9, and, in the Cotton Bowl, Texas, 20-14. And it handed Kentucky its only loss, 7-0, on Hank Lauricella's scoring pass in the regular season finale. No other team came within 2 touchdowns of Kentucky during the regular season.

Oklahoma was the only other team to defeat a tough Texas team. Billy Vessells and Leon Heath ran the Sooners to the first touchdown in the first 5 minutes of the game. Texas then dominated the following 50 minutes to take the lead, 13-7. Trying to punt, Bill Porter fumbled the ball to the Sooners on the Longhorns' 11. Vessels, a sophomore star who would become a Heisman hero in 1952, ripped through right tackle to make the tying touchdown. The great tackle Jim Weatherall place-kicked the winning point of a 14-13 thriller that left 75,000 fans in the Cotton Bowl deeply disappointed.

Oklahoma concluded the regular season with 31 consecutive victories and was voted the national titlist by both the AP writers' poll and the United Press International coaches' poll, which debuted this season. However, the voters did not have an opportunity to vote again following the New Year's Day postseason classics. And in the Sugar Bowl, Babe Parilli's passing and big Bob Gain's defense sparked the Wildcats to a 13-7 triumph. This ended the Sooner streak and earned Kentucky the right to claim the college crown, the first for Paul "Bear" Bryant.

There really was little to separate the top 3 teams of 1950. Each lost only 1 game. Tennessee beat Kentucky but was the only one to lose to a weak team. Kentucky lost to Tennessee.

Oklahoma lost to Kentucky. Bob Neyland said, "I always thought my 1938 team was my best ever, but now I'll never know because my 1950 team was just as good." However, the championship choice in the end came down to Kentucky and Oklahoma—and Kentucky beat Oklahoma. So that was that. Bear Bryant later said, "Kentucky was as entitled to the title as any team and I never had a better team."

However, Bud Wilkinson was really just beginning to roll with the powerhouse of the period at Oklahoma. He'd lost only 1 game in 1948 and none in 1949 and 1950. He felt entitled to claim the college crowns in both 1949 and 1950. After 3 frustrating seasons in which he would lose or tie 2 games, he put together perfect seasons in 1954 and 1955, which brought him 2 national titles in succession. He surpassed his earlier winning streak of 31 games in a row with a record 47 straight before being again beaten in 1957.

Again in 1951, the AP and UPI polls crowned a champion prior to the postseason play when the newly declared king was knocked right off the throne. Bob Neyland's next-to-last single-wing team at Tennessee, led by Lauricella and big Doug Atkins, swept through 10 straight rivals, clouting Kentucky, 28-0, to don the crown. Then it was knocked right off by Jim Tatum's mighty Maryland team, led by Jackie Scarbath, Bob Ward, Dick Nolan and Dick and Ed Modzelewski, 28-13, in the Sugar Bowl classic. Perfect in 10 starts, Maryland was the second school in a row to win what would be its only football title in history. It was recognized by selectors willing to wait for all the results.

Two other top-level teams had perfect campaigns. One was Charley Caldwell's Princeton team, paced by Dick Kazmaier, but it no longer competed in the big leagues. The other was Michigan State. Biggie Munn's Spartans knocked off 9 foes in a row, but were pressed by ordinary teams. Ohio State and

Indiana fell by 4 points each, Oregon State and Marquette by 6 each. Ohio State tied Illinois to mar Illinois's otherwise perfect record but lost or tied 5 games during the campaign. Georgia Tech was undefeated, but its record was marred by a tie with Duke.

Michigan State could claim at least a piece of the crown in 1951 and the whole thing in 1952, though Georgia Tech also was undefeated and untied this time around.

Bobby Dodd's Engineers downed a dozen rivals and handed Mississippi its only loss of the year in the Sugar Bowl, 24-7. The Tech team had no great players but was deep in good ones. However, Michigan State was virtually a unanimous title selection and ran its winning streak to 24 straight before that was snapped by a loss to Purdue, 6-0, the following season. The Spartans had a lot of little backs, including Don McAuliffe and Billy Wells, who ran wild in Munn's multiple-offense patterns. After Gene Lekenta's field goal with only 2 seconds left topped Oregon State, 17-14, State was seldom pressed and defeated Notre Dame decisively, among others.

Notre Dame was erratic in 1952 but did deal USC its only loss of the year, 9-0, in a typical season's end upset in this great traditional rivalry. USC ended another Oklahoma victory streak at 13 games, winning, 27-21, in the first nationally-televised college football contest.

By 1953, Leahy's last year, the Irish were ready to claim their leader's final college crown. Maryland was voted the AP and UPI titles because of its 10 straight triumphs in the regular season. However, after it was beaten by Oklahoma, 7-0, in the Orange Bowl, all the other selectors turned to the Irish, who went unbeaten—though tied by Iowa, 14-14.

The Irish, led by Ralph Guglielmi and Johnny Lattner, won 9 of 10, including 1 over Oklahoma, 28-21, which was the Sooners' only loss of the season. Forced to play both ways by new rules restricting substitutions and 2-platoon football this season, rules which would be weakened and gradually disappear over a period of 10 years, Guglielmi intercepted a pass, then threw one for 40 yards that defeated Oklahoma.

That was the first game of that season for the Sooners, who would not again lose for 47 games until another Notre Dame game 4 seasons later. Oklahoma, Ohio State and UCLA all went undefeated and untied in 1954. Red Sanders had constructed an old-fashioned single-wing powerhouse at UCLA. Aside from a 21-20 scare from Washington and a 12-7 scare from Maryland, the Bruins ripped through all their rivals, rolling up an average of 40 points per game. Operating behind a line led by Hardiman Curton, Jack Ellena and Jim Salsbury, tailback Primo Villanueva and fullback Bob Davenport routed rivals. Stanford, the only team to top UCLA the year before, was battered, 72-0. Archrival USC was smashed, 34-0.

In his fourth year at Ohio State, Woody Hayes put together his first top team and was entitled to claim a share of the national title, but State's performance was somewhat less impressive when the team got its shot at USC in the Rose Bowl, though winning, 20-7. The Buckeyes had a big line bulwarked by blocker Jim Parker and some splendid backs led by Hopalong Cassady, who became the last Big Ten star to win the Heisman by 1974. The Buckeyes beat 10 rivals in a row. At season's end, the AP poll picked them the top team in the country. UPI and most of the others went for UCLA, which is generally regarded as the title team of this season.

Curiously, no one went for Oklahoma, although the Sooners defeated 10 foes in a row and topped 300 points on offense. However, this sophomore-studded team was just hitting its stride, and all voters went for Bud Wilkinson's boys the next 2 years. They were the unanimous choices for the championship in both 1955 and 1956, putting together perfect records in 11 games in 1955 and 10 in 1956.

Behind the blocking of such as Jerry Tubbs, such swift runners as Tommy McDonald and Clendon Thomas sped to 380 points in 1955 and 466 points in 1956. The Sooners seldom passed, but they moved the ball. North Carolina was the only club to come close to Oklahoma in 1955, losing the opener, 13-6. After that the rest of the foes fell easily until postseason play. Maryland was the only undefeated, untied team to that time, but was shellacked by the Sooners, 20-6, in the Orange Bowl. This wrapped up the title for the winners. Colorado was the only club to come close to Oklahoma in 1956, losing at midseason, 27-19. The rest were routed. Oklahoma scored 35 or more points in every other game, 50 or more points 4 times and 60 or more points twice.

Notre Dame, which had lost only to Purdue in 1954 and only to Michigan State and USC in 1955, lost 8 games in 1956, including one by 40-0 to Oklahoma. This may have inspired new coach Terry Brennan's team to battle back in 1957 to win 7 games, including one by 7-0 over Oklahoma, which snapped the longest winning streak in the history of college football. However, Notre Dame was just another team by then, while the Sooners were the pigskin kings. That was the only game Oklahoma lost in 1957. In 10 seasons—from 1948 through 1957—Bud Wilkinson's Sooners lost only 7 games and had 4 undefeated seasons.

There were other good clubs in 1956. New coach Bowden Wyatt's Tennessee team went undefeated until beaten by Baylor, 13-7 in the Sugar Bowl. Led by Johnny Majors, the Vols dealt Georgia Tech its only loss of the year, 6-0. Forest Evashevski's Iowa eleven lost only to Michigan, 17-14. Bear Bryant had moved to Texas A&M, where his team did not lose a game but was tied by Houston, 14-14. This was a tough team, built around such rugged characters as John David Crow, Jack Pardee and Charley Krueger. But no club could compare to Oklahoma. Wilkinson's 1956 team was his topper, although he continued to coach through 1963.

Wilkinson was a wonder. He spent all 17 of his years as a head coach at Oklahoma, won 145 games, lost only 29, tied 4 and compiled a .729 winning percentage that stands as the seventh best ever. Although he played under Bernie Bierman at Minnesota, Wilkinson was shaped differently and taught a different brand of ball. A splendid, straight sort of person, soft-spoken and personable, Bud took a fatherly approach to his players and won their friendship off the field as well as their respect on it. A keen student of the game, he developed to perfection a split-T attack which stressed speed. His players struck sharply.

"I always wanted to win, but I wanted to have fun, too," he once said. "Once my players saw that winning was the most fun of all, they worked hard at it. I didn't drive them, but I didn't have to. You can motivate players better with kind words than you can with a whip." A handsome giant of a man, Wilkinson retired from coaching at the peak of his career to become a broadcaster and businessman and never returned despite tempting offers. After all, he never could have topped his success of the 1950s. He dominated his sport as much then as his old master had 30 or so years earlier.

If Bierman was thunder, Wilkinson was lightning.

10

Surge of the Southeast

OKLAHOMA APPEARED POISED to capture an unprecedented third straight national title when it hosted Notre Dame in the eighth game of the 1957 season before a homecoming crowd of more than 60,000 fans in Sooner Stadium. The Irish had been the last team to beat the Sooners, who had won 47 straight since, surpassing the 39 in a row Gloomy Gil Dobie wound up with at Washington in 1914. But the Irish had been beaten badly by the Sooners, 40–0, the year before, and beaten badly by Navy and Michigan in their preceding 2 games this year.

The crowd was roaring as the Sooners drove to the Irish 13-yard-line at the start of the game, then to the 32 a little later, but both times they were stopped, their sorties finished off on futile fourth-down passes. Suddenly, in the second session, Notre Dame started to move from midfield. Behind Bob Williams, the Irish blasted to the 3-yard-line. Four rushes later they were through on the 1-foot line. The teams went to intermission surprisingly scoreless.

An aroused Irish defense stalled the Sooners through the third period, but Clendon Thomas and David Baker uncorked punts that repeatedly pinned Notre Dame within its own 10-yard-line. The crowd could not believe Sooner lightning would not strike, but instead it was Irish magic that went to work. An Oklahoma punt landed in the end zone, permitting Notre

Dame to take over at its 20. The Irish mounted a march. It took 20 plays and used up almost all of the fourth and final quarter, but the Sooners could not contain it.

With Dick Lynch and Nick Pietrosante ripping through the line, Notre Dame reached the Oklahoma 7. Three line plunges produced only 4 yards. But the fourth-down play produced 6 points as Lynch faked another plunge, then rolled right, turned the end as surprised defenders dove desperately for him, and cut into the corner of the end zone. Monty Stickles place-kicked the extra point and it was 7–0.

Bud Wilkinson's boys tried to battle back. They got to their 34 and on fourth down tried to run for a first down and failed. Notre Dame took over. On fourth down the Irish gambled on a pass for a touchdown and failed. The Sooners got the ball back and surged to the Irish 24 in the last minute. Dale Sherrod's pass to tie in the last half-minute was intercepted by Williams in the end zone.

The Notre Dame players put Terry Brennan on their shoulders and trotted off in triumph, ·having handed the Sooners their first shutout in 123 games and their first defeat in 48. The Sooners and their fans departed in dejection. In the tomb-like Oklahoma dressing room, Bud Wilkinson sighed and said, "Well, we couldn't go on winning forever."

They went back to their winning ways the rest of the year, routing their remaining rivals—Nebraska, 32–7, Oklahoma State, 53–6, and, in the Orange Bowl, Duke, 48–21, but it was too late, the title had eluded them for this season.

The throne was moved from the midlands and sent south, where Southeastern Conference clubs would capture it 4 of the next 7 years and put in at least a claim to it all 7 seasons. Auburn was acclaimed national champion in 1957 and LSU in 1958. Mississippi claimed a piece of the crown in 1959 and the whole thing in 1960. Alabama earned it in 1961 and Ole Miss was back to claim a part of it in 1962.

Auburn boasted the only undefeated and untied record among major powers in 1957. Coach Ralph "Shug" Jordan's Plainsmen routed their state rival, Alabama, 40-0, but captured mostly close games on its defense. This was the best in the country. It permitted only 1 touchdown apiece to 4 rivals and blanked its 6 others. Auburn defeated Georgia Tech by 3-0, Georgia by 6-0, Kentucky by 6-0 and Tennessee by 7-0. Jimmy Phillips, Jackie Burkett and Zeke Smith played on Auburn's powerful line.

Auburn led the AP poll and most others. Ohio State won the UPI poll and a few others, but was beaten by TCU, 18-14, in its opener before beating its 9 remaining rivals. Linemen Jim Houston and Dick Schaffrath bolstered the Buckeyes, who barely beat Wisconsin by 16-13, Iowa by 17-13 and, in the Rose Bowl, Oregon by 10-7. This was a good Woody Hayes team, not a great one. It did not meet Michigan State, which lost only to Purdue in 9 games and had some championship support. (Purdue, which never has taken a title, has spoiled more championship hopes than any other non-champion over the years.)

Another Big Ten team, Iowa, was the only challenger to the class of the Southeastern Conference in 1958, but got only the Football Writers' Association trophy, while Louisiana State got all the rest. Iowa, led by Randy Duncan, had an offense but little defense. It won 8 wide-open games, but was beaten, 38-28, by Ohio State, and tied, 13-13, by Air Force.

Oklahoma would have won another title had it not been upset by Texas in what has become an outstanding early-season series. Texas had lost 6 straight and 9 out of 10 to

Oklahoma, but in his second season as the Steers' coach Darrell Royal had vowed to turn this traditional rivalry around. He started doing so on the second Saturday in October, 1958 in Dallas.

The big play was a gamble. Texas scored first on 2 passes from Bobby Lackey, one of 37 yards to Reni Ramirez and one of 10 yards to George Branch. The option of running or passing for 2 points after touchdown had been introduced into the college game as an alternative to the 1-point place-kick and Royal unexpectedly went for 2 and got them, Don Allen bucking over, for an 8–0 lead.

Oklahoma drove for a touchdown in the third period, but Wilkinson's try for a tie fell short as Bobby Boyd's pass fell incomplete. However, early in the fourth period Oklahoma took the lead when Jerry Thompson tackled Mike Dowdle so hard the ball popped free. Guard Jim Davis picked it out of the air and raced 24 yards to score. Boyd's pass to Jerry Tillery was good for 2 and the Sooners had surged in front, 14–8.

Texas took over on its own 24 and brought the ball downfield. Vince Matthews began completing short passes, including a fourth down pass to Bryant at one point, which the determined receiver carried through a tackle to a first down by inches at the Sooner 30. Matthews passed for 11 to Ramirez. Dowdle ran for 12. The Cotton Bowl crowd was roaring. First down on the 7. One run failed. Another. A pass missed. Fourth down. Lackey leaped up and fired a fast pass to Bryant, who, all alone in the end zone, caught the ball. Lackey then place-kicked the point. That made it Texas 15, Oklahoma 14.

In the waning moments, Lackey leaped to intercept a ball thrown by Boyd deep in Texas territory and the Steers were safe. The fans surged onto the field. Oklahoma's losers walked off sadly, their title hopes shattered.

Only one team went undefeated and untied in 1958. This was Louisiana State, coached by 34-year-old Paul Dietzel. As an assistant to Sid Gillman at Cincinnati 10 years earlier, Dietzel had given the name the "Chinese Bandits" to the second unit in an effort to instill special pride in the group. He coined it from the comic strip, "Terry and the Pirates," whose villains in the China-Burma area were especially unpleasant people. In 1958 offensive and defensive two-platoon units were curtailed by the rules, but teams could substitute entire units which could play both ways. Dietzel hoped to overpower the opposition with manpower. Rather than call his substitution team his second team he dug up the old nickname, the "Chinese Bandits." The unit battled to live up to the name and it caught public fancy.

There was more than publicity to this powerhouse, however. LSU had top players, including Warren Rabb, Johnny Robinson and a junior runner, Billy Cannon, who would win the Heisman Trophy a year later. Cannon was a game breaker. He scored on a 63-yard pass and a 25-yard run to spark a rout of Duke. He ran right at his rivals for 7 and 8 yards a clip in an iron-man demonstration during a drive that overcame Florida, 10-7. The big game was the seventh game, a meeting with also unbeaten Mississippi. The "Chinese Bandits" were brutal and Ole Miss was battered down, 14-0. Mississippi State actually was tougher, but was shaded, 7-6. In the Sugar Bowl, Clemson was overcome, 7-0. LSU had won 11 in a row and swept the AP and UPI polls.

One other Southeastern Conference club, Auburn, was unbeaten, but the Plainsmen were unsuccessful in defense of their national title because of a 7-7 tie with Georgia Tech. One eastern team, Army, was undefeated, but the Cadets were stymied by a 14-14 tie with Pitt. Another eastern team, Syracuse, had a splendid season spoiled by a 1-point upset at the hands of Holy Cross, then was ripped, 21–6, by Oklahoma in the Orange Bowl.

Ben Schwartzwalder was building a top team in upstate New York, and in 1959 Syracuse returned the East to the college throne for the first time since Army had ascended it 15 years earlier.

Syracuse had a strong team that compiled impressive statistics in winning 10 games in the regular season and an 11th, 23–14, over Texas in the Cotton Bowl. Only Penn State came close to the Orange, bowing 20–18. Syracuse led the country in both total offense, averaging more than 450 yards a game, and total defense, permitting less than 100 yards per game. No other team ever recorded such a sweep. The Orange also led in points with 413. Fullback Gerhard Schwedes scored an even 100.

However, the star was sophomore Ernie Davis, who ran for 141 yards against West Virginia and set a major bowl record by running a pass 87 yards to score against Texas. Before he was finished, Davis rushed for more than 2,300 yards, totaled 220 points and scored 35 touchdowns in his career to surpass the school standards set by Jimmy Brown a few years earlier. As a senior, Davis won the Heisman award.

After his graduation, it was discovered Davis had leukemia. He died less than 2 years later, never having had the opportunity to carry his career into pro ranks.

Syracuse was the only college club to compile a perfect record in 1959 and topped almost all the rankings. There was an odd vote here and there for Mississippi, which won 10 times but was upset by LSU, 7–3. LSU was thrown off the throne by Tennessee, 14–13. Washington won 10 times, but was stopped by Southern California, 22–15. Georgia won 10 times, but was stopped by South Carolina, 30–14.

The South shot back to the top in 1960. Mississippi merited

the title despite a 6-6 tie with LSU. Quarterbacked by Jake Gibbs, Johnny Vaught's Rebels won their other 10 games with only one close call, a 10-7 conquest of Arkansas, and climaxed the season with a 14-6 triumph over Rice in the Sugar Bowl.

No other top team in the nation went undefeated. The AP and UPI polls both went for Minnesota, but that was before the bowl games. The Football Writers' group and others went for Ole Miss. Minnesota did not merit the title, losing two of ten—23-14 to the old upsetter, Purdue, during the regular season and 17-7 to Washington in the Rose Bowl. Washington received some support but had lost to Navy, 15-14. Iowa had some support, too, but had been beaten by Minnesota, 27-10.

By 1961 the South was at or close to the top for the sixth straight season. That year Alabama was a near unanimous choice with 11 straight triumphs in which no team came within a touchdown of the Crimson Tide until they played Arkansas in the Sugar Bowl, winning by 10-3. Pat Trammel was the trigger-man of the offense, but the team's strength was in its defense, led by Lee Roy Jordan and Billy Neighbors, which shut out 6 foes—5 in a row—held 2 others to field goals and the other 3 to a single touchdown each. Tulane was topped, 9-0, Georgia Tech, 10-0, and Auburn, 34-0. This was the second national title for Bear Bryant.

Paul Bryant got his nickname not from being a bear of a man, which he is, but in his boyhood from wrestling a bear at a carnival. A big, gruff guy who recruits fervently, spoils his players off the field and pushes them on it, he favors small, fast teams. He is one who has won wherever he has coached, proving the point that poor programs can be rebuilt rapidly in this sport. Entering his 30th year as a coach in 1974, he had won 75 percent of his games, totalling 231 triumphs at

Maryland, Kentucky, Texas A&M and his alma mater, Alabama. His 1961 Crimson Tide may have been his best team.

'Bama had the only unbeaten, untied team in the country that year and topped all the polls except that of the Football Writers, who, strangely, went for Ohio State. The Buckeyes were the only other unbeaten team, but were tied in their opener by TCU, 7-7. They were impressive in a final 50-20 mauling of Michigan. TCU also spoiled the season for Texas, upsetting the Steers, 6-0. Another team whose season was spoiled in its opener was LSU, which lost to Rice, 16-3, before battling back to take 10 in a row, including a 10-7 defeat of defending champion Mississippi.

Mississippi returned with an undefeated, untied team in 1962, topping 10 straight opponents, including LSU and Tennessee and, in the Sugar Bowl, Arkansas, extending still further the southern reign in big-time college football, but it ended there for the time being because another undefeated, untied team that season, Southern Cal, was considered superior and swept all the annual awards.

11

Shift to the Southwest

JOHN MCKAY IS a modern man and has done much to remold the image of the college coach. He is a very funny man, perhaps the funniest coach in competition. He has a spontaneous wit and he is honest about his feelings. He doesn't say his team will lose if he feels it will win. He doesn't say a foe is good if he thinks it is bad. He is not afraid to speak his feelings.

Criticized for having O. J. Simpson carrying the ball so much one season, the Southern Cal coach shrugged and said, "Why not? He doesn't belong to a union. The ball isn't very heavy, anyway." When another runner stumbled and fell shortly after taking the opening kickoff of a contest, McKay turned to an assistant on the sidelines and screamed, "My God, they've shot him."

McKay is not a pal to his players, but he also doesn't preach to them. "Football is only a part of their lives. You have to keep it in perspective," he observes. After a 51-0 humiliation at the hands of Notre Dame, he did not go into the dressing room and dress down his players, nor did he hide out. He told his team, "Don't worry men, there are 500 million Chinese that will never know the difference." Threatening not to show up for the rematch the following season and told he would then be a loser by forfeit, 2-0, McKay observed, "Well, that'd be 49 points better than we did last year." His team won, 24–7. "That's even better," he smiled later.

He admits he hides behind his fast tongue. "I don't want to make excuses, but I have to face the press. If I can give 'em a fast line, they'll take it and go away with it and leave me alone." He considers coaching tougher than playing. He says disappointing defeat does not stay with a player as long: "He has other interests. He goes to a party. He goes out with a girl. He escapes. But the game is the coach's life. He takes it home with him. There's no escape for him."

Born poor in depression days in West Virginia, he played alongside Norm van Brocklin at Oregon and stayed on as an assistant coach. He went to USC as an assistant and a year later became head coach.

Recruiting is the roughest part of a coach's job in college. He competes with others trying to talk top talent into attending his school. It is a demeaning, demanding task and McKay handpicks supersalesmen as aides who can corner the best prospects from his fortunately fertile area. "You can't win without top players, but you can lose with them," he notes. He doesn't lose a lot.

The Pacific Coast Conference had been split asunder by penalties imposed due to alleged illegal payments to players, and McKay came in to rebuild the once-proud program at USC and show the way back to the top to other far-western universities. An imaginative, inventive tutor, he assembled tremendous teams that never quit. From 1962 through 1972 his teams made 3 marches to the national title.

His 1962 team had 2 top quarterbacks, Pete Beathard and Bill Nelson, and strong runners in Willie Brown and Ben Wilson. It featured a great receiver in Hal Bedsole and a host of powerful linemen, including Damon Bame and Marv

Marinovich. It captured 10 straight games during the regular season, defeating Duke, 14-7; Iowa, 7-0; Navy, 13-6; UCLA, 14-3, and Notre Dame, 25-0, among others.

The Trojans had lost 11 games in McKay's first 2 seasons, but they skyrocketed to the top in his third campaign. Willie Brown, now a USC assistant coach comments, "He'd been building and he got us to believing in ourselves." Brown made an incredible catch of a pass from Nelson that proved decisive in the UCLA game. "He got it up and I got up to it," Brown recalls. "It came at the right time. Later teams here have had better talent, but that was a gutty bunch of guys who made the big plays and never quit under pressure."

The Rose Bowl proved the point. Wisconsin, whipped only by Ohio State all season, proved a true test. USC's stunning offense swept to a 28-7 halftime advantage. Bedsole boosted it to 35-7 on a 57-yard pass play in the third quarter. After Ron VanderKelen passed for a Badger touchdown, Bedsole hauled in another scoring toss to build the edge back to 42-7 early in the fourth quarter.

Wisconsin then went wild as 102,000 spectators in the ancient arena in Pasadena went wild, too. VanderKelen, who completed 33 of 48 passes in an awesome aerial display during the day, filled the late afternoon air with footballs. As the arc lights were turned on to meet the evening, he threw for 4 touchdowns within 12 minutes before USC took over and froze the football in the final 2 minutes to preserve a 42-38 edge. It was one of the wildest and most exciting games in collegiate history.

This brought USC its first national title since the days of Howard Jones' 30 years before. Mississippi also compiled a perfect record, and after stopping Arkansas in the Sugar Bowl had the right to claim a share of the laurels. Alabama could have done so, too, except for a 7-6 upset by Georgia Tech. But the stronghold of football was shifting from the Southeast to the Southwest.

Texas, which was unbeaten and untied until a 13–0 loss in the Cotton Bowl to LSU, and Arkansas, which lost only 2 games in 1962, were ready to rise to the top.

Texas got there first, in 1963. A former student of Bud Wilkinson's at Oklahoma, Darrell Royal headcoached at Mississippi State 2 years and Washington one before taking over at Texas. In his sixth season there, he scaled the heights after several earlier near misses. Like his mentor, Wilkinson, and like Bear Bryant, Royal put a lot of his best talent on defense and stressed swiftness on offense, preferring quick strikers to size and a running game to a passing one. Frank Broyles at Arkansas, who became Royal's keenest rival, played the same game.

The full-scale return of two-platoon football was still 2 seasons away, but substitution rules were being liberalized year by year so that by 1963 Royal could overwhelm opponents with numbers. He had recruited a lot of good players, mostly from his football-crazed state, and had 2 great ones, tough tackle Scott Appleton and one of the leading linebackers of all time, Tommy Nobis.

Texas routed a lot of rivals, including Oklahoma, in 1963. It also just slipped past some stiff foes. Arkansas was beaten by 17–13, SMU by 17–12, Texas A&M by 15–13, Rice by 10–6 and Baylor by 7–0. But Texas established itself as the best this season when it ran roughshod over Roger Staubach's Navy team in the Cotton Bowl classic, 28–6. Navy had lost only to SMU, 32–28, and had the highest-scoring team in the country and one of its best of recent seasons. It was returning to the postseason bowl scene for the first time in many years, but it was no match for Texas.

As the only undefeated team in the country, Texas was the unanimous choice as the college champion.

In 1964 Arkansas ascended the throne after taking a thrilling tilt from Texas when a daring gamble by Royal failed.

Ken Hatfield took an Ernie Koy punt 81 yards behind a wave of blockers along the left sideline for the first score. Tom McKnelly kicked the conversion and Arkansas led, 7–0, at halftime. The third period was scoreless. Then the action erupted.

Early in the final period, Koy keyed a 46-yard drive climaxed when Phil Harris rushed over from the 2 and David Conway place-kicked the point to tie the contest.

A penalty on a punt for having an extra player on the field cost Texas the ball near midfield and gave Arkansas a first down on its own 30. Arkansas went all the way as Fred Marshall flung the ball 34 yards to Bobby Crockett, who took it into the end zone on the run. McKnelly's kick made it 14–7.

With more than 65,000 fans filling its home stadium with sound, Texas marched dramatically from its own 3-yard-line the length of the field in the final minutes. The Steers reached the Razorback 12, but were thrown back 5 yards on 3 plays.

Facing a fourth and 15, Texas got the distance cut in half as Arkansas was penalized because a Hog had grabbed a face mask in making a tackle. From here, fullback Hal Phillips shot to the 1 for a first down. Koy cut across and it was 14–13.

Here Royal had a difficult decision to make. His kicker, Conway, had not missed a conversion all season, and one more would tie the game. But Royal later admitted, "We want to win, not tie. The only decision I had to make was not whether to go for 1 or 2 points, but which way to go for the 2, by run or pass. Either is tough, but from the 3 the pass is a better bet."

He lost. Marv Kristynik rolled left, tore free from a tackler, let fly fast and threw the ball behind Hix Green, who was wide open in the end zone. A little more than a minute was left.

Arkansas took the kickoff and ran 2 plays, hanging on to the ball. The gun sounded. Broyles, a brilliant tutor out of Georgia Tech, was swept up on the shoulders of his players and out of the stadium in triumph.

As Royal observed, "Well, as Bear Bryant said, 'A tie is like kissing your sister.' If we were willing to settle for a tie, we wouldn't play in the first place. That'd be the safe way not to lose. If you play, you risk losing." Losing the only game his team lost all year, Royal and Texas lost their national title. Arkansas wrapped it up by beating Nebraska in the Cotton Bowl, 10-7.

Notre Dame lost only to John McKay's gutsy USC team, which rallied dramatically in the last minutes to nip the Irish, 20-17. Michigan lost only to upsetter Purdue, 21-20. Alabama lost only to Texas, 21-17, in the Cotton Bowl. It already had received the AP and UPI awards, but that was before the bowls. After them, the rest went to Arkansas, the only unbeaten and untied team in the country in 1964.

So Texas, which had beaten Arkansas in the last minute in 1962, 7-3, fell short in the last minute in 1964, 14-13. But in 1969 Royal would gamble against Arkansas again and win, 15-14, and with it another unanimous national title. No one in the 1960s played football more fiercely than these southwest terrors.

12

The Midwest on the Move

ONCE WHEN JOHN McKAY's team was concluding a disappointing campaign, he had to give a speech at a school banquet and he brought all his assistant coaches with him. "Take a good look at these men," he told his audience. "Everyone knows we get the best talent. And everyone knows I'm a good coach. Someone must be responsible for failure. So this may be the last time you see these men."

Duffy Daugherty's mind turns in the same directions. At the end of a championship season, he spoke at a banquet at Michigan State. "I've been asked to make a speech about my football team," he said, "my team that just won nine games, my team that just won the Rose Bowl, my team that . . ." He paused, eyeing his audience. "I'm sorry," he said. "I forgot this isn't my football team. It's really yours. Last year when we only won three games it was mine."

Duffy was one of the new breed of college coaches. He wanted to win, but if he couldn't have fun doing it he felt it wasn't worth it. Football was a game to him, not a holy crusade. He recognized that it was a hard game. "Football isn't a contact sport," he said. "Dancing is a contact sport. Football is a collision sport." But he befriended his players and was beloved by them. He was one of the boys. Once when his team was under tremendous pressure, he pulled a prank to relieve the tension. He asked a cop to arrest one of his players on the practice field. When the cop captured the player, the lad and his teammates were stunned.

"What did I do?" the lad asked.

"You've been stealing cereal from the training table and taking it home to your family," Duffy informed him.

The laughter relaxed the team, which went on to win. Duffy's teams won because he knew how games should be played and got his players to play them his way. If he had been more dedicated to perfection he might have won more titles for his teams and more laurels for himself, but as it was he put together one of the top teams of all time at Michigan State in 1965 and 1966, which won or shared in both national titles. In 75 years there haven't been 10 teams which could claim back-to-back championships.

No clubs compiled perfect records in 1965. Alabama lost its opener to Georgia, 18-17, then was tied by Tennessee later, 7-7. Nebraska, Arkansas and Michigan State were perfect through the regular season, but bowed in bowl games. Alabama knocked off Nebraska in the Orange Bowl, 39-28. LSU knocked Arkansas off the national throne in the Cotton Bowl, 14-7. Michigan State, which had defeated UCLA in its first game, 13-3, lost to UCLA in its last game, the Rose Bowl, 14-12.

Before the bowls, the AP voted for Alabama, UPI went for Michigan State and the Football Writers group declared the title a tie between the two. But all the other selectors, before and after, went for Michigan State. Both Michigan State and Alabama had lost 1 game, but Alabama also had tied one. The Spartans merited the title. They beat Michigan by 17 points, Penn State by 23 and Ohio State by 25. They knocked off Notre Dame, 12-3. Only Purdue came within a touchdown of them until postseason play and State thwarted the upsetter, 14-10.

The UCLA loss could not be disregarded, but Tommy Prothro's team was tough. Gary Beban's bombs led to a 14-0 lead. Daugherty's Spartans rallied for 2 touchdowns. He gambled on 2-point plays. With 7 minutes left. Bob Apisa tried to punch over but Jerry Klein nailed him short of the goal line. With half a minute left, Apisa tried to skirt right end, but little Bobby Stiles bounced him back. Stiles was knocked unconscious with the force of his leaping tackle, but so were Spartan hopes. The Rose Bowl rocked with cheers.

Michigan State had a star-studded team sparked by quarterback Jimmy Raye, running back Clint Jones, offensive end Gene Washington, defensive end Bubba Smith and defensive back George Webster. In 1966 it did not lose a game. Neither did Notre Dame. But they tied and split the seasonal laurels. Strangely, the AP, UPI and almost all other selectors chose the Irish as champion, so they must be considered the king of the year, though a few gave the Spartans pieces of the prize as they were equally deserving.

Ara Parseghian had arrived from Miami of Ohio and Northwestern to inherit the reins once held by greats at Notre Dame. He swiftly restored the school's proud image in his first season, 1964. He won every game but one. In that one, he led USC at halftime, 17-0. Led by the passing of Craig Fertig and the running of Mike Garrett, the Trojans rallied to within 17-13. Late in the last quarter, the Trojans drove 60 yards to score. On fourth down, with 2 minutes to play, Fertig passed to Rod Sherman in the end zone to win, 20-17, in one of the most compelling comebacks in college annals.

Parseghian brought the Irish back in 1966. They had a lot of talent, led by quarterback Terry Hanratty, running back

Nick Eddy, offensive end Jim Seymour, offensive guard Tom
Regner, defensive tackle Pete Duranko and linebacker Jim
Lynch. They shut out 7 of their 10 foes. They scored 362
points. No one came within a touchdown of them until they
came up to Michigan State in their next-to-last game of the
season. The defending national champions had edged Ohio
State by 3 points and knocked off 8 other rivals by 2 touchdowns or more. This was their last game.

It was a classic contest, widely publicized and awaited, and
a terrific struggle before an overflow crowd of more than
80,000 fans in Spartan Stadium and millions more watching
on national television. Michigan State marched 73 yards to a
touchdown, and Dick Kenney, a barefoot kicker from Hawaii,
shot the Spartans in front, 10-0, with a conversion and a 47-
yard field goal before the Irish roared back. Big Bubba Smith
had sidelined Irish quarterback Terry Hanratty with a violent
tackle, but sub Coley O'Brien came in to throw a 34-yard
scoring pass to Bob Gladieux to make it 10-7 at intermission.

The second half developed into a tense defensive struggle.
The Irish penetrated Spartan territory midway in the half, but
settled for Joe Azzaro's 28-yard field goal to tie it, 10-10, on
the first play of the last period.

After that, Daugherty sent his Spartans to gamble daringly
for a game breaker, while Parseghian put his Irish in a shell.
One Spartan gamble gave the Irish a crack at a 41-yard field
goal with 4 minutes left, but it missed. Another, an interception of a Jimmy Raye pass by Tom Shoen, was returned
to the Spartan 17, but 4 plays failed, the fourth a pass
deflected in the end zone.

With 75 seconds left, Notre Dame got the ball back on its
own 30, but O'Brien, on orders, simply took the ball from
center, held on to it and plowed straight ahead into the line 3
straight times to run out time. Boos bombarded the Irish. So
the big game ended in a disappointing deadlock.

Later, Daugherty laughed and said, "When you're playing for the national championship, it's not a matter of life and death, it's more important than that."

Parseghian said, "I didn't want to risk giving it to them cheaply. I wasn't going to do a jackass thing like throw it away at that point."

The wisdom of Parseghian's strategy was established when, after the Irish roared out to rout USC, 51-0, the next Saturday in their concluding contest, Notre Dame generally was acclaimed as college champions for the first time since the late 1940s, a quarter century earlier.

Neglected was another Alabama array, coached by Bear Bryant to an undefeated and untied season. Quarterbacked by Ken Stabler, anchored on defense by Bobby Johnson, the Crimson Tide shut out 6 foes, 4 in a row, edged past Tennessee, 11-10, and routed 10 other foes, including Nebraska in the Sugar Bowl.

Georgia lost only to Georgia Tech while UCLA lost only to Washington. Aside from its 51-0 loss to Notre Dame, USC lost, 14-7, to UCLA and 14-13, to Purdue in the Rose Bowl in its last three outings of 1966, but bounced back behind the spectacular O. J. Simpson to bring John McKay his third national title in 1967.

The Trojans had a tremendous defense built around Tim Rossovich, linebacker Adrian Young and defensive back Mike Battle. They had brilliant blockers led by giant tackle Ron Yary. They had a swift end in Earl McCulloch. And a strong one in big Bob Klein. And they had Simpson, who may be the best running back ever to play the game.

O. J. emerged from a San Francisco junior college to play 2 seasons at Southern Cal. In these 2 seasons he surpassed the standards set previously by almost all 3-year performers. McKay wasn't afraid to make him work. The strong, swift Simpson ran 266 times for 1,415 yards and 11 touchdowns as a junior and 355 times for 1,709 yards and 22 touchdowns as a senior. He was awesome.

He was surrounded by more talent as a junior than he was as a senior and so his side was more successful in 1967 than it was in 1968, though it came close to capturing the national title both years.

USC decisively defeated most of its rivals in 1967. It survived 2 tough early tests, topping Texas, 17-13, and Michigan State, 21-17. It got revenge on Notre Dame, 24-7. It slipped only once, in the mud at Oregon State, losing, 3-0.

Simpson ran for 150 yards against Notre Dame for 158 yards against Texas and for 190 yards against Michigan State. Despite a sprained arch, he slipped through the mud for 188 yards at Oregon State. He was at his best against the best.

Following the loss to Oregon State, USC surrendered the Number 1 ranking in the polls to crosstown rival UCLA and returned home to take on UCLA in the biggest game this great traditional rivalry ever has produced. UCLA had been tied by Oregon State, but there was not an undefeated and untied team in the country. This USC-UCLA classic was for the national title.

No other city has 2 such sporting powers, much less has any ever had 2 playing for the national championship. And the stars, Simpson and UCLA's Gary Beban, were Heisman Trophy rivals. More than 90,000 partisan spectators crammed into the Los Angeles Coliseum to see the game of the year, if not the century. And this game lived up to its advance notices as few ever have.

In the beginning, the Bruins were in charge. Greg Jones ran for a 7-0 lead. But on the last play of the first period, Beban underthrew a pass, Pat Cashman picked it off and went 55 yards to tie the contest. The Bruins drove back to the Trojan 15, where Beban's sore ribs were bruised and he had to be bound up tightly. Zenon Andrusyshyn failed on a field-goal try and USC took over.

Earl "The Pearl" McCulloch sped 52 yards to put the Trojans in position to score. Simpson ran 15 yards through 6 tacklers to put his side in front, 14-7. Beban, breathing hard beneath taped ribs, completed one pass for 48 yards to Dave Nuttall before the Bruins stalled. Andrusyshyn tried another field goal, but it was blocked by Bill Hayhoe, a 6-8 giant inserted by McKay for this.

After intermission, Beban bombed George Farmer for 55 yards and the tying score. Late in the third quarter, another Andrusyshyn field-goal bid was blocked by Hayhoe again. Into the fourth quarter they went. Beban moved his team 65 yards to a 20-14 lead, but this time it was the conversion kick Andrusyshyn couldn't get by Hayhoe.

Simpson, despite his sore foot, started to move. On third and eight from his own 56, he finally broke free. He faked to his right, swerved to his left, angled to the middle, shedding tacklers as he went, faked out the final defender and fled 64 yards into the end zone. "The thrill of it," wrote one writer, "will live to the last day of the last man alive who saw it."

The Coliseum was coming apart with the roars of the rival rooters. Then, amid a sudden hush, Rikki Aldridge place-kicked perfectly his third straight extra point, the tie was broken and USC had won, 21-20.

Beban won the Heisman, but Simpson and his side won everything else, and the next year he got the Heisman, too. USC was acclaimed king of the gridiron for 1967 even before it trimmed Indiana, 14-3, with Simpson starring in the Rose Bowl on New Year's Day.

Oklahoma, returning to the top under the coaching of Chuck Fairbanks, led by a bull of a back, Steve Owens, was the only other contender with a record worthy of title consideration. The Sooners lost only to Texas, 9-7, in a typically tough traditional meeting. However, USC captured both the AP and UPI polls and almost all the rest, too.

The Trojans had a real shot at it again in 1968. With Simpson stronger than ever, they avenged themselves on Oregon State, 17-13, and downed UCLA, 28-16. Simpson ran 47 times for 238 yards against Oregon State and 40 times for 205 yards against UCLA. The Trojans had a perfect record until tied by Notre Dame, 21-21, in their regular season finale. This was McKay's mistake. Simpson was run only 20 times and settled for a career-low 55 yards.

Still, the Trojans had a shot at the national title when they went into the Rose Bowl against Ohio State, one of 2 other undefeated teams in the country. Simpson rushed 28 times for 171 yards and caught 8 passes for 85 more yards. His dazzling 80-yard scoring run helped USC to a 10-0 lead. But then Simpson and the Trojans started to fumble and make mistakes, and the big, bruising Buckeyes got back into it. Directed artfully by Rex Kern, they ground out one long drive after another and won going away, 27-16.

USC was really not very far from winning 3 in a row. The following year they snatched a 14-12 victory from UCLA and trimmed Michigan, 10-3, in the Rose Bowl, but a 14-14 tie with Notre Dame spoiled their otherwise perfect record and cost them the crown.

With his Rose Bowl romp over USC, Woody Hayes hung on to the 1968 laurels. He may not be lovable. He hollers a lot and growls when he isn't hollering. He pushes his players through punishing private practices. He refused to permit them to speak to the press. He, himself, seldom speaks to the press. He has been known to jam a photographer's camera right into his face. He may not coach an exciting style of football. It consists primarily of a grudging defense and a grind-it-out offense. His fullbacks smash center again and again and again. But he can coach this sport.

Hayes seldom has superstars, but he gets as many good players as anyone and overpowers the opposition with manpower. He stresses fundamentals and his men seldom make mistakes. His best player in 1968 was a big blocker, tackle Dave Foley, and his defense was shakier than usual, but his nameless men mauled every rival in a series of high-scoring contests for one of 5 national titles he has won or shared. The Denison, Ohio, graduate and former Denison and Miami of Ohio coach entered 1974 with 192 triumphs in 28 years as a coach and a winning percentage of .754. "I'd rather be respected than loved," he growled.

One coach who would like a little more respect is Joe Paterno. Paterno also had an undefeated and untied team at Penn State in 1968. He had splendid players, including Ted Kwalick and Jack Ham. The Nittany Lions trimmed 10 straight rivals, including UCLA, and got by Kansas, 15–14, in the Orange Bowl, but because they play in the East among teams that no longer contend for national honors they are neglected when the crowns are passed around. It happened again when Paterno put together other undefeated and untied teams in 1969 and 1973.

He has said, "It is an injustice." And he is right. He and his school are entitled to claim at least shares of these crowns. Entering 1974, Paterno had won 75 games in 8 seasons as a coach and his .848 winning percentage was much the best among active mentors. He had put together undefeated streaks of 23 and 31 games—despite the fact that his team's accomplishments have gone largely unrewarded.

Paterno's 1969 Penn State team, bulwarked by a tremendous tackle, Mike Reid, swept all 11 starts, including a 10–3 victory snatched from Missouri in the Orange Bowl. But the Nittany Lions were overshadowed by Texas, the only other undefeated and untied team in the country and Darrell Royal's second team to be acclaimed national champion unanimously.

"You say I'm one of only three men in modern times ever to coach two unanimous national champions in college football? Who're the others? Red Blaik and Frank Leahy? Well, that's just fine. I don't put myself in a class with them. I'm just a country boy trying to get along," Royal told this writer.

In 1969, he had no stars but a lot of fine players. Until their tenth game, no team came closer than 10 points to them and they ran up point totals of 45, 49, 49, 56, 56 and 69 on their rivals.

The last game of the regular season was something else, that traditional rivalry with Arkansas. Bill Montgomery's passes to Chuck Dicus carried the Razorbacks to a 14-0 lead after 3 quarters. History tells us these big games are never over until the gun sounds and that is the way this one was.

The fans were whooping it up for the home side when the visitors hushed them. On the first play of the last quarter Jim Street went back to pass, was trapped by tacklers, squirmed free and fled 42 yards to score. Royal who had been burnt by a 2-point gamble against this team a few years earlier, gambled again and won, Street sneaking across to cut the deficit to 14-8.

Arkansas took the kickoff and sought to tuck the victory away. Montgomery moved the Razorbacks on passes to Dicus for 20 yards and 27 yards and one to Johnny Rees for 14. Dancing around against the rush, he drove his rooters wild. Then he had Dicus open in the end zone and threw for him, but Danny Lester cut in front of the receiver and picked off the pass to return the ball to Texas.

The touchdown and even the insurance field goal were gone

now, and soon the victory would be, too. With 6 minutes left, the Steers marched. On fourth down at the Texas 43, Royal gambled again and Street sent Randy Peschel deep downfield and hit him on the fly for 44 yards. Bedlam broke out. From the 13, Ted Koy knifed to the 2. Jim Bertelsen then rammed over guard to tie the game. Happy Feller kicked the extra point and Texas led, 15–14.

Arkansas rallied in the last minutes, but Tom Campbell intercepted a pass 20 yards from his goal line at the end and tumbled to the ground with the ball, the game and the college crown grabbed to his breast. Texas protected the honors by coming from 10 points behind to knock off Notre Dame, 21–17, in the Cotton Bowl in Dallas.

One hundred years after the first game of intercollegiate football was played, a dramatic contest for the national title served as a suitable celebration.

13

Recent Kings

As COLLEGE FOOTBALL turned into the 1970s and toward 75 years of more or less officially crowning national champions, it took the postseason bowl games to settle the first title of the new decade.

Ohio State entered New Year's Day ranked number 1 and seeking its tenth consecutive conquest of the 1970 season. It was heavily favored over a Stanford team which had lost 3 games, including its last 2.

However John Ralston's Cardinals arrived at the Rose Bowl with the Heisman Trophy winner, Jim Plunkett, and a lot of spirit. While Woody Hayes kept his club confined in southern California, Ralston's players partied, visited Disneyland and relaxed.

Plunkett's passes set Stanford up for a 10–0 lead early in the game. Aroused, just as they had been in the 1969 Rose Bowl contest that clinched that title for them, the Buckeyes then rallied to take command on long marches climaxed by short runs by John Brockington to go in front, 14–10.

However, whereas Ohio State had then pulled away from USC in the earlier classic, they could not put the Stanford team away this season. After an exchange of field goals to make it 17–13, Ohio State's "three yards and a cloud of dust" offense carried the club to fourth and a foot at the Stanford

19. A foot figured to be a soft touch for the Buckeye muscle, but Stanford rose up to bounce Brockington back.

Inspired by the California crowd cheering them on, Stanford moved the ball deep into Ohio State territory. Seemingly stalled at third down, 16 yards to go on the 35, Plunkett scrambled under a rush and threw deep down the right sidelines where Bobby Moore took the pass to the 2. From here, Jackie Brown rolled around right end to score and the Bucks were broken.

Soon afterwards, Jack Schultz picked off a pass from Rex Kern at the State 25 and 4 plays later Plunkett threw 10 yards for a touchdown to Randy "The Rabbit" Vataha and the Bucks were buried, 27-17, their title dreams dashed.

Meanwhile, in Dallas, Texas took the opening kickoff in the Cotton Bowl 78 yards in 4 plays to a field goal and a 3-0 lead, but Notre Dame knifed them down by scoring touchdowns the first 3 times they had possession.

Joe Theissman threw a 26-yard touchdown pass to Tom Gatewood for the first one, then ran for the next 2 after his throws set them up. Royal's defending national champions marched to a touchdown to cut the count to 21-11, but Ara Parseghian's Irish rolled right back with a drive to a field goal that sapped the spirit from the Steers.

The second half was filled with fumbles and was scoreless. The dream of a second straight and unprecedented third unanimous national laurel for Royal and his Texas team was finished, 24-11.

Meanwhile, in Miami, in the Orange Bowl, Bob Devaney's Nebraska team, a running team all season, turned to the pass to propel it past LSU, 17-12. Jerry Tagge completed 5 passes on a first-quarter series which led to a field goal by Paul Rogers. Before the period ended, a fumble recovery by Willie

Harper set up a short run by Joe Orduna to a touchdown and a 10-0 lead.

LSU rallied with 2 field goals, then went ahead, 12-10, on a 31-yard pass from Buddy Lee to Al Coffee late in the third quarter. More than 80,000 fans were hollering for the South, but the Cornhuskers took the kickoff 67 yards on 14 plays to a fourth-quarter score taken in by Tagge. Nebraska hung on to the game and the national title. Ranked third behind Ohio State and Texas going in, Nebraska left with its players hollering, "We're number 1."

They were, too, despite a 21-21 tie with USC in the second game of their season. No other top power went undefeated. Arizona State did, but did not compete on the top level. USC, a spoiler this season, had knocked off Notre Dame, 38-28, in the last game of the regular season. Then Notre Dame knocked off Texas in the Cotton Bowl. When Stanford finished off Ohio State in the Rose Bowl, Nebraska had its first national title, although UPI had voted for Texas before the bowl results were in.

It was not Nebraska's last title. They became one of those rare teams to win 2 in a row, taking 13 games in a row in 1971 when every other major club lost at least once. Oklahoma lost only one, but that was the big one, to Nebraska, in a nationally televised Thanksgiving Day contest that was an offensive classic. The Sooners had lost, 28-21, to the Cornhuskers in 1970 and they lost a 35-31 thriller to them this time.

Oklahoma was geared to check Nebraska breakaway artist Johnny Rodgers, but in the fourth minute, little, agile Rodgers fielded a punt on his own 28 and went all the way. Oklahoma coverage was excellent and the Nebraska star probably should have called for a fair catch, but he was a daring guy.

Right off, he was hit by his All-American rival, Greg Pruitt. Rodgers spun away, stumbling for balance, found it, and discovered he had been shoved free of the oncoming defenders by the collision. He took off to his left behind blocker Joe Blahak, got the block he needed and sped 72 yards down the sidelines to a 7-0 lead.

An Oklahoma field goal cut it to 7-3 at the quarter. Nebraska's Tagge marched his side downfield and Jeff Kinney knifed across from in close to make it 14-3. Then Jack Mildren, the Oklahoma quarterback, went to work. He ran for one touchdown, passed for another and suddenly at halftime Oklahoma led, 17-14.

In the third period Tagge took the Huskers to 2 scores, both bucked across by Kinney, and Nebraska was back on top, 28-17. Before the quarter ended, however, Mildren ran for his second touchdown. Then in the final quarter he passed for his second and Oklahoma led, 31-28, and the 63,000 fans were limp at the ebb and flow of furious action.

Time was short when Nebraska made a last move to extend its undefeated string to 29 straight contests. Kinney tore 17 yards through 3 tacklers, then another 13 through 3 more. In trouble, third and eight on the Oklahoma 46, Tagge faded to pass, was pressured out of the pocket, ran from rushers, spotted Rodgers downfield and threw for him. Rodgers squeezed between 2 bigger men, got the ball, dropped to one knee and hugged the pigskin on the 35 to keep his side alive.

From the Oklahoma 6, with 2 minutes to play, Tagge called on Kinney, who crashed for 4, then for 2 for his fourth touchdown. With the conversion it was 35-31 with less than 2 minutes left. Oklahoma couldn't come back and Nebraska was on its way to another college crown.

It was wrapped up in the Orange Bowl when second-ranked Alabama was ripped from the ranks of the undefeated and untied on a 77-yard scoring punt return by Rodgers on the last play of the first quarter, sparking the Huskers to a 38–6 romp. They captured every single first-place vote in the AP poll.

The laurels were long overdue at Nebraska, one of the nation's pioneer powers in college football, and long overdue for coach Devaney, a patient man who waited out 14 years as a high-school coach before he got his chance at college coaching as an aide to Biggie Munn, then Duffy Daugherty at Michigan State, before going on to Wyoming and winding up at Nebraska.

A graduate of little Alma College in Michigan, which also gave the world the coaching of George Allen, Devaney made football fun for his players with his soft touch and wide-open offense. But he developed powerful teams. When he retired after the 1972 season, he led all active coaches with a winning percentage of .806 on 136 victories, only 30 losses and 7 ties in 16 seasons, which put him in the top ten all-time.

At Nebraska, he lost only 20 games in 11 seasons. His longest unbeaten streak, 31 games, was snapped in the first game of the following year by UCLA, 20–17, and Nebraska was never in the title chase after that. The Huskers beat Army, 77-7; Missouri, 62-0; Kansas State, 59-7, and Kansas, 56-0; but a 17-14 loss to Oklahoma in the finale sealed a disappointing season for a strong team, whose star, Rodgers, won the Heisman Trophy.

Oklahoma lost only to Arkansas, 14–13, in 1972, but Chuck Fairbanks' spectacular team was forced to forfeit 3 victories later when it was learned quarterback Kerry Jackson had been recruited irregularly. Oklahoma did not lose any games in 1973, but was tied, 7-7, by USC. By then, however, the Sooners had been placed on probation by the NCAA for having in the school and on their team 2 players whose high-school transcripts had been altered.

Oklahoma was prohibited from participating in postseason classics and in 1974 the coaches who voted in the UPI poll had decided not to vote for Oklahoma, no matter what the Sooners did during the season.

The Sooners were caught breaking the rules. In such cases, however, the violations often are the work of one or two men, maybe a sympathizer or an assistant, without the consent of school officials. And it is not clear that many more schools who were not caught had not broken or at least badly bent the rules in the intense chase for the college championship.

In any event, Oklahoma's loss in 1972 and tie in 1973 would have been sufficient to cost them those crowns because USC and Notre Dame went undefeated and untied in turn in those seasons. USC coach John McKay, whose club won him his third national title in 1972, was one who agreed with the elimination of a school from contention for the crown while it was on probation.

"If a school has broken the rules it should be deprived of any benefits it might gain by its act," observed the usually affable mentor. "It is not fair to spread the impression we all break the rules. We don't. I don't. I am accused of it because I win, but all schools and especially winners are constantly investigated and we have been declared clean time and time again."

He smiled and said, "I win because I get good players and good assistant coaches and I'm a good coach. We want to win because everyone wants to win whenever he plays any kind of game. . . . All of life is a quest for victories of some sort, in love, war and work, and if you don't lay it on the line to your lads you're not telling them the way it is.

"We don't always win. No one does. Sometimes our players aren't good enough and sometimes my coaching isn't good enough. The other players may be better in a given game or a given season. Or the other coach. But we win our share. And if we do lose, we don't pretend it's the end of the world.

"I don't agree with critics of the polls that they put too much pressure on the players. The polls aren't always accurate, but they attract interest to our sport and fill our stadiums, and they are as fair as they can be. They're truer now that the results of bowl games are added on. Now we're measured over our full seasons.

"A national championship tournament of some sort might be a big thing, but I'm against it because I believe it would destroy the bowls and I believe the bowls have been the best thing to ever happen to football. They give teams goals. We shoot for our conference first every season, because if we win it we'll go to the Rose Bowl and we look on that as our reward for our season's hard work. But we are always shooting for the national championship, too."

He sat at a training table surrounded by the young giants who made up his latest team and said, "A lot of luck enters into winning the championship of college football. They rate you before the season even starts, based on the previous season's results and the new season's potential, and if you start off number 1 and win all your games you're going to finish number 1. If you don't start off number 1 you have to hope the teams ahead of you lose so you can move up when you win. It helps if you schedule the top teams because the best way to move up is to beat the teams ahead of you. Penn State has had some great teams, but hasn't been voted number one because it never meets the team that is number one or number two or number three.

"If you lose early, you're probably licked. You drop so far down so fast they may forget you no matter what you do the rest of the year. After you're established at the top or near the top of the polls you may be able to afford a defeat. It all depends on whether the other teams lose at least once. When we were voted number one in 1962, we weren't the only un-defeated team but we impressed the voters more than Mississippi. When we were voted number one in 1967, we lost one game, but everyone else lost at least one more too and again we made the best impression. Maybe it was because of Simpson. Maybe because our uniforms were prettiest. Maybe because I'm so charming. Who knows?

"There's a lot of luck in it. It helps to be at home for your toughest games, for example. It helps to avoid injuries in your key positions and to your key players. From year to year the teams that may be the strongest may not come out on top, but the team that wins deserves it because one way or another it got the job done. My 1972 team was the best of my national championship teams because it didn't have a close game all year and was a unanimous choice as number one. It had fair talent, but above all it was superbly coached."

Asked, he said, "It also was the best team I've ever seen. They say those old teams coached by the old masters such as Howard Jones were marvelous machines, but I've seen some films and I can tell you they make more mistakes and did less than the top teams today. They were the best of their day so they deserve their trophies, but the game has come a long way and teams play a lot better today."

His hair gone white, the cigar-chewing coach laughed: "Hey, I'm proud of having won three national championships. Not many have. But I'm at a school where football is popular. Our games make a lot of money and we can afford the sort of program that can produce a national championship team like our 1972 team. Some schools seem afraid to stress sports. Hell, our school is as good scholastically as any. I think a winning sports program is something every school should seek.

"I'm not misplacing my values. Winning boosts school spirit and keeps the alumni close to the school, and they're the people that pitch in with the money that keeps a school strong. Football supports our entire sports program and makes it self-sufficient. Everyone wants to associate with a winner. You get complaints when you lose, you know. Not when you win," he grinned.

The Trojans won them all in 1972. They had a tremendous amount of talent topped by sophomore running back Anthony Davis, fullback Sam "Bam" Cunningham, flanker back Lynn Swann, tight end Charley Young, offensive tackle Pete Adams, defensive tackle John Grant and linebacker Rich Wood. On consecutive Saturdays they ripped Arkansas, 31-10; Oregon State, 51-6; Illinois, 55-120, and Michigan State, 51-6. Stanford held them to 30-21, but was the only team to come that close to them all season. Traditional rival UCLA was wiped out, 24-7. It was not until the tenth and last game of their regular season that the Trojans were defeated.

This was the renewal of their spectacular series with Notre Dame. Davis brought the Coliseum crowd of more than 75,000 fans to its feet by returning the opening kickoff 97 yards through swarms of tacklers to score. The Trojans built a big lead, then eased off. The Fighting Irish fought back, closed to 25-23 and seemed to be moving on momentum toward an upset. Following the last Irish touchdown, however, Davis took the kickoff and raced 96 yards through the entire Irish team for his second scoring return of the game, electrifying the crowd and ruining the visitors. He also ran for 99 yards from scrimmage and scored 6 touchdowns in what wound up a 45-28 romp.

Oklahoma had knocked Nebraska and Texas from the

running, and had in turn been knocked out of the race by Colorado. Ohio State had beaten Michigan and stood between USC and the 1972 national title in the Rose Bowl on New Year's Day 1973. But the Buckeyes were blasted by the Trojans, 42-17, as Davis ran for 157 yards and Cunningham leaped the line for 4 touchdowns. Not only did USC get to add all the title trophies and other silverware to its display cases in Heritage Hall, but they got all 50 first-place votes in the AP poll.

The following season, 1973, was somethig else again. Davis, concealing cracked ribs, was almost as efficient but not as effective. The Trojans could not get their talent together. They tied a tough Oklahoma team but then at midseason were nailed by Notre Dame and at the end of the season slaughtered by a vengeful Ohio State club in the Rose Bowl, 42-21. Ohio State already had been removed from the running by a tie with Michigan.

The Big Ten title and sometimes the national title had been coming down to this season-end traditional meeting of Ohio State and Michigan for several seasons. Ohio State was upset by an inspired Michigan eleven by 10-7 in the 1971 spectacular. Ohio State upset Michigan by 14-11 in the 1972 thriller. The Buckeyes of Woody Hayes and the Wolverines of Bo Schembechler entered the 1973 finale undefeated and untied and contending for the college crown. An NCAA regular-season record of more than 105,000 persons packed the Ann Arbor arena, which annually contributes the country's top crowds to the more than 30,000,000 fans who watch college football each season now.

The Buckeyes were favored and broke on top, 10-0, on the hard running of Archie Griffin behind the blocking of big John Hicks. But Schembechler coaches clubs that keep coming at rivals. By season's end he had averaged 8 victories a year and a .783 winning percentage in 11 years as a coach, which made him third only to the .793 of Arizona State's Frank Kush and the .848 of Penn State's Joe Paterno among active mentors. He didn't win this one, but he came close.

Schembechler knew Hayes' Buckeyes not only would not but could not pass effectively, so he threw almost everyone up front and stalled the visitors in the second half. Meanwhile quarterback Cornelius Greene and fullback Ed Shuttlesworth got the Wolverines on the move.

Shuttlesworth carried on 8 of 11 plays that led to a 30-yard field goal by Mike Lantry early in the fourth quarter. Franklin then passed 27 yards to Paul Seal, and, after faking to Shuttlesworth, sneaked 10 yards to score the tying touchdown. Lantry, who made the critical conversion, had a near miss from 58 yards out and a bad miss from 34 yards out in field goal efforts in the gathering gloom as the game ended dramatically deadlocked, with the fans in the stadium and in front of their television sets spellbound by the contest, which spoiled the season on both sides.

Only Penn State, Alabama and Notre Dame concluded the campaign undefeated and untied and meriting national title recognition. Joe Paterno put together another team at Penn State which proceeded perfectly through its schedule, but the Nittany Lions did not face a foe that finished in the top ten, so that eliminated them, though they certainly could claim they were number 1 with no one having proven otherwise.

However, it came down to that wide-open Orange Bowl battle between Notre Dame and Alabama to decide the championship of college football for 1973. Ara Parseghian said, "We always go after the national title. Why not? We don't belong to a conference. We want to win every game." And, after a high-scoring struggle that thrilled the thousands in Miami and millions in their living rooms across the country, it was settled by a field goal in the fading moments that won it for Notre Dame by the sheerest of margins, a single point, 24–23, over Alabama. This made the Fighting Irish once again what they had been more often than any other team over the many years of this sport—the one thing every team wants to be: Number 1.

A wild scramble ensued for the college crown of the 1974 season and the climactic contest again was a postseason battle between Notre Dame and Alabama, this time on New Year's night in the Orange Bowl in Miami.

Ohio State, Penn State, Michigan, Notre Dame, Alabama, Oklahoma, Texas and Southern Cal were the outstanding contenders for the crown. In the end only Oklahoma concluded the campaign undefeated, but that did not settle the controversy.

Placed on probation by the NCAA for recruiting violations, Barry Switzer's Oklahoma club was permitted to play through the regular season in competition for conference honors, but barred from television appearances and postseason bowl bids.

Controversially, the coaches voted to exclude the Sooners from national championship consideration. Those coaches who participated in the UPI poll did not vote for them throughout the season.

However, the writers and broadcasters who participate in the AP poll included Oklahoma in their consideration, and the Sooners led most of the season and wound up number 1 by a whopping margin when the final balloting was taken at season's end. They won 51 of the 60 first-place votes.

Their 1973 title hopes stalemated by a tie with USC, Oklahoma compiled a perfect record in 1974, sweeping 11 foes. They had an explosive offense sparked by end Wayne Hoffman, tackle Jerry Arnold, guards John Roush and Terry Webb, and All-American running back Joe Washington.

They had a deadly defense led by All-American linebacker Rod Shoate, Jimbo Elrod, Randy Hughes and the Selmon brothers, LeRoy and Dewey.

The Sooners scored 483 points and surrendered only 92. They averaged almost 44 points a game, shut out 3 foes and allowed no team more than 2 touchdowns. They routed Utah State, 72–3; Wake Forest, 63–0, and Kansas State, 63–0. They crushed such capable rivals as Colorado by 49–14, Kansas by 45–14, Oklahoma State by 44–13 and Missouri by 37–0. They beat Baylor, 28–11; Nebraska, 28–14; Iowa State, 28–10, and topped Texas, 16–13.

It was a representative schedule as Oklahoma State, Nebraska, Baylor and Texas all were selected for postseason bowl games.

The toughest test for Oklahoma was posed at Texas. Darrell Royal's disappointing Texans, who struggled through an uneven season, scored a touchdown and 2 field goals to take a 13–7 lead early in the last quarter. A 40-yard end-around run by Billy Brooks tied it, but a missed conversion kick left it tied. However, when the Longhorns gambled on a fourth-and-1 at midfield and were stopped short, the Sooners drove and prevailed on a 37-yard field goal by Tony Rienzo in the waning minutes.

Defending national champion Notre Dame was upset in its third game by the old spoiler, Purdue, 31–20, and barely beat 4 soft foes by a touchdown or less in its first 10 games. Penn State was upset by Navy early and North Carolina State late. Ohio State swept 8 straight before being upset by Michigan State in a controversial contest. Trailing, 13–3, the Spartans surged spectacularly to a 16–13 lead on a 44-yard scoring pass play, Charlie Baggett to Mike Jones, and an 88-yard scoring run by Levi Jackson in the final period.

Ohio State drove to avert defeat. Cornelius Green's pass

was intercepted by linebacker Terry McClowry, but one official overruled another in declaring it no interception. Game films showed it to be an interception. Given a new lease on life, the Bucks battered to the Spartan 1 with 25 seconds to go and no time-outs left. The Bucks tried to set up for a play. Time ran out as the ball was snapped. Greene fumbled it, but Champ Henson scooped up the loose ball and hammered home. However, officials ruled time had run out before the ball was snapped.

A harried Hayes protested to no avail, the final ruling arriving from Big Ten boss Wayne Duke a half hour later in support of the officials. No matter, the call was no worse than the one that had deprived the Spartans of a saving interception a few plays earlier.

Meanwhile Michigan was moving along mightily and its mammoth stadium was packed for home games. Michigan drew 104,682 fans for the Michigan State game and 104,232 fans for a Navy game, totals topped in regular-season attendance only by a turnout of 105,223 for Michigan's 1973 Ohio State game.

Michigan and the Big Ten led the nation in attendance, although the national total of more than 31 million fans at games of 634 college football teams was fractionally less than the previous season, the first season in many that there was not an increase.

On New Year's Day 1975, Ohio State and USC drew 106,721 to their Rose Bowl game in Pasedena, which fell only 148 fans short of their modern record postseason total in the same match 2 years earlier.

Ohio State and USC returned to the Rose Bowl by winning critical late-season contests—Ohio State field-goaling its way to a 12–10 triumph over Michigan and USC routing cross-city rival UCLA, 34-9.

Bo Schembechler's balanced Michigan Wolverines got past 10 straight teams, beating Michigan State, 21-7, and walloping Purdue, 51-0, along the way, before bowing in a heartbreaker to Woody Hayes's Buckeyes in the regular-season finale, which has settled the Big Ten title and Rose Bowl bid in recent seasons.

Meanwhile, John McKay's USC Trojans had their record spoiled in a 22-7 loss at Arkansas in the season opener and a 15-15 tie with California at midseason. Arkansas wound up losing 4 games and tying a fifth, while Cal lost 3 and tied a fourth.

Illogically, however, Southern Cal was reinstated in the championship picture when it concluded its campaign with a 55-24 rout of Notre Dame in the regular-season finale and an 18-17 upset of Ohio State in the postseason Rose Bowl classic.

The nationally televised Notre Dame game may have been one of the most astonishing games in gridiron history. Notre Dame roared to a 24-0 lead before Southern Cal scored just before halftime to cut the count to 24-7.

Another spectacular scoring return of a kickoff, 100 yards long, by dynamite Anthony Davis touched off a 48-point second half explosion by Southern Cal that buried their rival unbelievably.

Student athlete Pat Haden, selected for a Rhodes Scholarship to Oxford, picked apart the opposition with pinpoint passes, many of them to the coach's son, Johnny, deeply disappointing the Fighting Irish and their coach, Ara Parseghian, who shortly announced his retirement from the collegiate ranks.

The Rose Bowl was billed as a battle between junior Archie Griffin, the winner of the Heisman Trophy balloting, and senior Davis, the runnerup. However, Davis, an almost incomparable clutch runner, was injured and missed most of the game after first-half heroics, while the hard-running Griffin was held to less than 100 yards rushing for the first time in 23 games, just as he had been held below 100 by another band of Trojans in the '73 Rose Bowl.

For a while, defensive All-Americans Neil Colzie and Pete Cusick contained the Trojans while Corny Greene, the star of the '74 Rose Bowl, led the Buckeyes into a 17–10 lead.

A perfect pass from 38 yards out into the end zone—Haden to McKay, a boyhood buddy and high-school teammate—with 2:03 to play, lifted the Trojans to within 17–16 Then the elder McKay passed up a place-kick for a tie and went for the win with Sheldon Diggs diving to grab Haden's pass just above the ground for the decisive 2 points. A 62-yard field goal bid by Buckeye Tom Skladany fell just short at the gun and one of the great games was history.

Southern Cal may have been the best team in the country at season's end. Swept up in a wave of emotion, UPI coaches voted the Trojans the national title after Notre Dame bade Parseghian goodbye with a 13–11 outlasting of Bear Bryant's Alabama team that night in Miami. Southern Cal also was selected for the Grantland Rice Trophy and the MacArthur Bowl. But few teams ever have been regarded as deserving of the title after failing to win 2 games, and USC's slips marred these awards. Failing to win only one and losing to better teams, Alabama and Michigan had superior records. But the best record of all was Oklahoma's, which would have been happy to risk it in a bowl if permitted.

Alabama came through several close calls to win all 11 of its regular-season contests and was on its way to a share of the championship, but the fired-up Irish took advantage of 'Bama mistakes to take a 13–3 halftime edge in the first half and hung on, despite a long, late strike by the Crimson Tide, to prevail. It was the eighth straight season Alabama had failed to win a postseason bowl outing and was a bitter blow to Bryant.

Logically, it left Oklahoma the 75th national college champion of modern American football. Permitted to play, they should be allowed the laurels they earned. However, there remain many who feel John McKay entitled to a fourth crown with Southern Cal. So, as it almost always has been, the collegiate title was claimed in controversy.

Claimants to the National Crown

1900

Yale (12–0–0)	Handed Harvard only loss.
Clemson (6–0–0)	Southern foes inferior at time.
Minnesota (8–0–1)	Tied by Iowa.

1901

Michigan (11–0–0)	Routed Stanford in first Rose Bowl.
Harvard (12–0–0)	Dealt Yale only loss.
Wisconsin (9–0–0)	Did not meet Michigan.

1902

Michigan (11–0–0)	Gave up 1 TD in 2 years.
Yale (11–0–1)	Handed Harvard lone defeat. Tied Army.
Nebraska (10–0–0)	Unscored on. Trimmed Minnesota.

1903

Princeton (11–0–0)	Gave up only 1 TD, to Yale.
Minnesota (14–0–1)	Tied by Michigan.
Michigan (11–0–1)	Co-champ of Midwest.
Nebraska (10–0–0)	Second straight perfect season.
Notre Dame (8–0–1)	Scoreless tie with Northwestern.

1904

Minnesota (13–0–0)	Scored on by only 1 foe.
Michigan (11–0–0)	Won 1 game 130–0.
Penn (12–0–0)	Won series of defensive duels.
Pitt (10–0–0)	Also an eastern power.
Vanderbilt (9–0–0)	One of the new powers.
Auburn (7–0–0)	New southern power.

1905

Chicago (9–0–0)	Nosed out Michigan and Wisconsin.
Stanford (8–0–0)	Contender from Far West.
Yale (10–0–0)	Survived scare from Harvard.
Penn (12–0–1)	Tie spoiled season.
Princeton (9–0–1)	No undefeated, untied contenders.

1906

Yale (9–0–1)	Tied Yale.
St. Louis (11–0–0)	Upstart from Midwest.
Utah (6–0–0)	Undefeated and unscored on.

1907

Yale (9–0–1)	Tied by Army. Nipped Princeton.
Dartmouth (8–0–1)	Upset Harvard.
Marquette (6–0–0)	Surrendered only 4 points.

1908

Penn (11–0–1)	Tied by Carlisle.
Harvard (9–0–1)	Tied by Navy.
Chicago (5–0–1)	Tied by Cornell.
Kansas (9–0–0)	Undefeated Midwest entry.
LSU (10–0–0)	Tainted by charge of professionalism.
Auburn (6–0–0)	Loss to LSU wiped from record.

1909

Yale (10–0–0)	Unscored on.
Washington (7–0–0)	Pacific Coast contender.
Arkansas (7–0–0)	Tops in Southwest.
Notre Dame (7–0–1)	Scoreless tie with Marquette.

1910

Washington (6–0–0)	Still class of the Pacific Coast.
Harvard (8–0–1)	Scoreless tie with Yale.
Pitt (9–0–0)	Unscored on.
Arkansas (8–0–0)	Still Southwest's topper.
Illinois (7–0–0)	Also unscored on.
Navy (8–0–1)	Scoreless tie with Rutgers.
Vanderbilt (7–0–1)	Tied Yale.

1911

Carlisle (11–1–0)	Pop Warner's mighty Indians.
Washington (7–0–0)	Third straight perfect season.
Princeton (8–0–2)	Tied by Lehigh and Navy.
Penn State (8–0–1)	New eastern threat.
Minnesota (6–0–1)	Tie marred mark.
Oklahoma (8–0–0)	Early scourge of Southwest.

1912

Harvard (9–0–0)	Dealt Yale only loss.
Notre Dame (7–0–0)	Nipped Pitt.
Wisconsin (7–0–0)	Beat Minnesota and Chicago.
Penn State (7–0–0)	Scored on by only 1 foe.

1913

Notre Dame (7–0–0)	Dorais to Rockne through the air.
Harvard (9–0–0)	Trimmed Yale.
Chicago (7–0–0)	Topped Purdue in big game.
Washington (7–0–0)	Seventh straight title in Far West.
Auburn (8–0–0)	Class of South.
Nebraska (8–0–0)	Mighty in Midwest.
Michigan State (7–0–0)	Moving up to contend.

1914

Illinois (7–0–0)	Trimmed Minnesota and Chicago.
Army (9–0–0)	Sunk the Navy.
Tennessee (9–0–0)	Best in the Deep South.
Texas (8–0–0)	Class of the Southwest.
Washington & Lee (9–0–0)	A power at this time.

1915

Pitt (8–0–0)	Topped Penn, routed Navy.
Cornell (9–0–0)	Beat Harvard and Michigan.
Nebraska (8–0–0)	Nosed out Notre Dame.
Washington (7–0–0)	Took 2 from California.
Oklahoma (10–0–0)	Awed Alma, 102–0.

1916

Army (9–0–0)	Knocked off Notre Dame.
Pitt (8–0–0)	Nosed out Navy by a point.
Ohio State (7–0–0)	First big Buckeye club.

1917

Georgia Tech (9–0–0)	Third straight season unbeaten.
Pitt (9–0–0)	Also third straight undefeated year.
Texas A&M (8–0–0)	New Southwest contender.
Washington State (6–0–0)	Rose to top in Far West.

1918

Pitt (4–0–0)	Despite war-reduced schedule.
Texas (9–0–0)	Trimmed Texas A&M.
Virginia Tech (7–0–0)	New power in South .

1919

Texas A&M (10–0–0)	Edged Army and Nebraska.
Notre Dame (9–0–0)	Unscored on. Topped Texas.
Harvard (9–0–1)	Tied by Princeton.
Centre (9–0–0)	"The Praying Colonels."

1920

California (9–0–0)	"The Wonder Team."
Notre Dame (9–0–0)	Rockne's crew unbeaten again.
Texas (9–0–0)	Nipped Texas A&M.
Harvard (8–0–1)	Tied by Princeton again.
Princeton (6–0–1)	Stalled Harvard title drive.
VMI (9–0–0)	Won 136–0 and 96–0 games.

1921

Iowa (7–0–0)	Ended Notre Dame's 20-game winning streak.
Cornell (8–0–0)	Won one by 110–0.
Lafayette (9–0–0)	Topped Pitt and Penn.
Wash. & Jeff. (10–0–1)	Tied Cal in Rose Bowl.
California (9–0–1)	Unmarked until bowl failure.

1922

Cornell (8–0–0)	Second straight perfect campaign.
Princeton (8–0–0)	Nosed out Yale, 3–0.
California (9–0–0)	Third straight undefeated season.
Iowa (7–0–0)	Second straight perfect season.

1923

Illinois (8–0–0)	Red Grange's debut year.
Michigan (8–0–0)	Allowed only 1 TD.
Cornell (8–0–0)	Third perfect record in row.
Yale (8–0–0)	Topped Harvard and Army.
SMU (9–0–0)	Allowed only 9 points.
Marquette (8–0–0)	Foes ordinary.
Colorado (8–0–0)	Schedule weak.

1924

Notre Dame (10–0–0)	Led by "The Four Horsemen."
Dartmouth (7–0–1)	Tied by undefeated, twice-tied Yale.

1925

Alabama (10–0–0)	Edged Washington in Rose Bowl.
Dartmouth (8–0–0)	Hammered Harvard.

1926

Navy (9–0–1)	Tied by Army.
Stanford (10–0–1)	Tied by Alabama in Rose Bowl.
Alabama (9–0–1)	Second straight unbeaten campaign.
Lafayette (9–0–0)	Outpointed Pitt.

1927

Texas A&M (8–0–1)	Scoreless tie with TCU.
Illinois (7–0–1)	Upset tie by Iowa State.
Army (9–1–0)	Nosed out by Yale.
Yale (7–1–0)	Beaten by Georgia.
Georgia (8–1–0)	Beaten by Georgia Tech.

1928

Georgia Tech (10–0–0)	Wrong-way Riegel's run helped.
USC (9–0–1)	Tied by California.
Tennessee (9–0–1)	Scoreless tie with Kentucky.
Detroit (9–0–0)	Strong Midwest team.

1929

Tulane (9–0–0)	Nipped Texas A&M.
Notre Dame (9–0–0)	Topped USC by a point.
Purdue (8–0–0)	Just got by Iowa.

171

1930

Notre Dame (10–0–0)	Nipped Army by a point.
Alabama (10–0–0)	Just got by Kentucky.

1931

Tennessee (9–0–1)	Tied by Kentucky.
USC (10–1–0)	Lost opener to St. Mary's.
Tulane (11–1–0)	Trimmed by USC in Rose Bowl.
Purdue (9–1–0)	Lost to Wisconsin.
Pitt (8–1–0)	Lost only to Notre Dame.

1932

USC (10–0–0)	"The Thundering Herd."
Michigan (8–0–0)	Captured close contests.
Colgate (9–0–0)	Outscored foes 264–0.
Tennessee (9–0–1)	Scoreless tie with Vanderbilt.

1933

Princeton (9–0–0)	Allowed only 1 touchdown.
Michigan (7–0–1)	Scoreless tie with Minnesota.
USC (10–1–0)	Scoreless tie with Oregon State.

1934

Alabama (10–0–0)	Stunned Stanford in Rose Bowl.
Minnesota (8–0–0)	Handed Pitt only loss of season.

1935

Minnesota (8–0–0)	Won the tight ones.
Princeton (9–0–0)	Topped Penn by a point.
SMU (12–1–0)	Upset by Stanford in Rose Bowl.

1936

Northwestern (7–1–0)	Beat Minnesota, lost to Notre Dame.
Minnesota (7–1–0)	Won first Associated Press Poll.
Pitt (8–1–1)	Lost to Duquesne. Tied by Fordham, 0–0.
Alabama (8–0–1)	Tied by Tennessee.

1937

Pitt (9–0–1)	Tied by Fordham, 0–0, again.
Fordham (7-0-1)	Tied by Pitt.
California (10–0–1)	Tied by Washington.
Santa Clara (9–0–0)	Defeated LSU in Sugar Bowl.

1938

Tennessee (11–0–0)	Defeated Oklahoma, Sugar Bowl.
Texas Christian (11–0–0)	Defeated Carnegie Tech, Cotton Bowl.
Duke (9–1–0)	Unscored on until 7–3 USC Rose Bowl loss.
Notre Dame (8--1–0)	Defeated by USC.

1939

Texas A&M (11–0–0)	Defeated Tulane in Sugar Bowl.
Cornell (8–0–0)	Defeated Ohio State.
Tennessee (10–1–0)	Lost to USC.

1940

Stanford (10–0–0)	Popularized T-formation.
Minnesota (8–0–0)	Won 2 games by 1 point each.
Boston College (11–0–0)	Weak schedule until bowl game.
Tennessee (10–1–0)	Lost to BC in the Sugar Bowl.

1941

Minnesota (8–0–0)	Topped Northwestern by 1 point.
Notre Dame (8–0–1)	Scoreless tie with Army.
Duke (9–1–0)	Lost only in Rose Bowl to Oregon State.

1942

Georgia (9–1–0)	Upset by Auburn. Won Rose Bowl.
Ohio State (9–1–0)	Upset by Wisconsin.
Tulsa (10–1–0)	Lost Sugar Bowl to Tennessee.

1943

Notre Dame (9–1–0)	Lost to Great Lakes All-Stars.
Purdue (9–0–0)	Played easier schedule.

1944

Army (9–0–0)	Wartime powerhouse.
Ohio State (9–0–0)	Beat Michigan by 4.

173

1945

Army (9–0–0)	Continued to demolish all foes.
Alabama (10–0–0)	Beat USC in Rose Bowl.
Oklahoma A&M (9–0–0)	Stopped St. Mary's in Sugar Bowl.
Indiana (8–0–1)	Tied by Northwestern.

1946

Notre Dame (8–0–1)	Tie ended Army unbeaten streak.
Army (9–0–1)	Scoreless tie with Irish.
Georgia (11–0–0)	Won Sugar Bowl from North Carolina.

1947

Michigan (10–0–0)	Routed USC, 49–0, in Rose Bowl.
Notre Dame (9–0–0)	Defeated by Northwestern.

1948

Michigan (9–0–0)	Extended by Michigan State.
Notre Dame (9–0–1)	Tied by USC.
Army (8–0–1)	Tied by Navy.
Clemson (11–0–0)	Nipped Missouri in Sugar Bowl.

1949

Notre Dame (10–0–0)	Survived SMU scare.
Oklahoma (11–0–0)	Tight fits with Texas and Santa Clara.
Army (9–0–0)	1-pointer over Penn.

1950

Oklahoma (10–1–0)	Upset by Kentucky, but won first UPI poll.
Kentucky (11–1–0)	Topped by Tennessee.
Tennessee (11–1–0)	Lost early to Mississippi State.

1951

Maryland (10–0–0)	Beat Tennessee in Sugar Bowl.
Tennessee (10–1–0)	Lost only to Maryland.
Michigan State (9–0–0)	Nosed out Ohio State and Indiana.
Georgia Tech (11–0–1)	Tied by Duke.

1952

Michigan State (9–0–0)   Nosed out Oregon State.
Georgia Tech (12–0–0)   Edged Florida and Alabama.

1953

Notre Dame (9–0–1)   Upset tie by Iowa.
Maryland (10–1–0)   Lost to Oklahoma in Orange Bowl.
Oklahoma (9–1–1)   Lost to Notre Dame, tied by Pitt.

1954

UCLA (9–0–0)   Nipped Washington by a point.
Ohio State (10–0–0)   Three close victories.
Oklahoma (10–0–0)   Barely topped Texas and TCU.

1955

Oklahoma (11–0–0)   Stretched streak to 30 wins.

1956

Okla'ioma (10–0–0)   Again only perfect team.

1957

Auburn (10–0–0)   Won 5 close contests.
Ohio State (9–1–0)   Lost opener to TCU.
Michigan State (8–1–0)   Topped by Purdue.

1958

LSU (11–0–0)   "The Chinese Bandits,"
Oklahoma (10–1–0)   Lost by 1 point to Texas.
Army (8–0–1)   Tied by Pitt.
Iowa (8–1–1)   Lost to Ohio State, tied Air Force.

1959

Syracuse (11–0–0)   Only undefeated contender.
Mississippi (10–1–0)   Upset by LSU.

1960

Mississippi (10–0–1)	Tied by LSU.
Missouri (10–1–0)	Lost to Kansas.
Washington (10–1–0)	Lost to Navy.
Navy (10–1–0)	Lost to Duke.
Iowa (8–1–0)	Lost to Minnesota.
Minnesota (8–2–0)	Lost to Purdue and Washington.

1961

Alabama (11–0–0)	Nipped Arkansas in Sugar Bowl.
Ohio State (8–0–1)	Tied by TCU in opener.

1962

USC (11–0–0)	Whipped Wisconsin in Rose Bowl.
Mississippi (10–0–0)	Nipped Arkansas in Sugar Bowl.

1963

Texas (11–0–0)	Only undefeated contender.

1964

Arkansas (11–0–0)	Edged Texas and Nebraska.
Alabama (10–1–0)	Lost to Texas.
Notre Dame (9–1–0)	Lost to USC rally.
Michigan (9–1–0)	Lost by point to Purdue.

1965

Michigan State (10–1–0)	Split 2 games with UCLA.
Alabama (9–1–1)	Lost to Georgia, tied by Tennessee.
Arkansas (10–1–0)	Lost to LSU in Cotton Bowl.
Nebraska (10–1–0)	Lost to Alabama, Orange Bowl.

1966

Notre Dame (9–0–1)	Tied by Michigan State.
Michigan State (9–0–1)	Shaded Ohio State.
Alabama (11–0–0)	Topped Tennessee by one point.

1967

USC (10–1–0)   Upset by Oregon State.
Oklahoma (10–1–0)   Topped by Texas.

1968

Ohio State (10–0–0)   Stopped USC in Rose Bowl.
Penn State (11–0–0)   One-pointer in Orange Bowl over Kansas.

1969

Texas (11–0–0)   Nipped Arkansas by a point.
Penn State (11–0–0)   Beat Missouri in Orange Bowl.
USC (11–0–1)   Tied by Notre Dame.

1970

Nebraska (11–0–1)   Tied by USC.
Texas (10–1–0)   Upset by Notre Dame in Cotton Bowl.
Ohio State (9–1–0)   Lost to Stanford in Rose Bowl.
Notre Dame (10–1–0)   Lost to USC.
Tennessee (11–1–0)   Upset by Auburn.

1971

Nebraska (13–0–0)   Only undefeated contender.

1972

NSC (12–0–0)   Rose Bowl rout of Ohio State.

1973

Notre Dame (11–0–0)   Beat Alabama by a point.
Ohio State (10–0–1)   Rose Bowl rout of USC.
Michigan (10–0–1)   Tied Ohio State.
Oklahoma (10–0–1)   Tied by USC.
Penn State (12–0–0)   Held back by schedule.

1974

Oklahoma (11–0–0)   On probation, no bowl game.
USC (10–1–1)   Rose bowl upset of Ohio State.
Alabama (11–1–0)   Orange Bowl upset by Notre Dame.

177

All-time Top College Teams

(Through 1974)		(Through 1973)	
Team	**Victories**	**Team**	**Percentage**
Yale	666	Notre Dame	.774
Princeton	613	Yale	.760
Harvard	605	Princeton	.770
Penn	602	Michigan	.736
Michigan	568	Texas	.723
Notre Dame	563	Alabama	.717
Texas	544	Harvard	.705
Alabama	512	USC	.705
Penn State	502	Oklahoma	.700
Dartmouth	498	Tennessee	.697
Ohio State	497	Ohio State	.693
Army	492	Army	.683
Tennessee	494	Dartmouth	.676
Nebraska	491	Penn State	.670
Oklahoma	485	Miami (Ohio)	.662
USC	477	Minnesota	.652
Cornell	467	Nebraska	.659
Minnesota	464	LSU	.649
Syracuse	461	Penn	.646

Leading Title Teams

Teams	Titles (Arbitrary)	Titles and Shares	Teams	Titles (Arbitrary)	Titles and Shares
Notre Dame	11	19	Ohio State	1	9
Michigan	4	11	Harvard	1	6
USC	4	9	Washington	1	5
Alabama	3	10	Cornell	1	5
Oklahoma	3	10	Auburn	1	4
Pitt	3	9	Arkansas	1	4
Yale	3	8	Iowa	1	4
Minnesota	3	8	California	1	4
Army	3	8	Mississippi	1	3

Teams	Titles (Arbitrary)	Titles and Shares	Teams	Titles (Arbitrary)	Titles and Shares
Princeton	3	7	Chicago	1	3
Tennessee	2	8	Penn	1	3
Michigan State	2	7	Navy	1	3
Texas	2	6	Texas A&M	1	3
Nebraska	2	6	Georgia	1	3
Georgia Tech	2	5	LSU	1	2

Teams	Titles (Arbitrary)	Titles and Shares	Teams	Titles (Arbitrary)	Titles and Shares
Illinois	2	3	Maryland	1	2
			Stanford	1	2
			Kentucky	1	1
			UCLA	1	1
			Tulane	1	2
			Carlisle	1	1
			Northwestern	1	1

Others Who Shared In Titles: Dartmouth 3, Purdue 3, Duke 2, SMU 2, Lafayette 2, Wisconsin 2, Vanderbilt 2, Marquette 2. ONE EACH—St. Louis, Utah, Kansas, Washington and Lee, Washington & Jefferson, Washington State, Virginia Tech, VMI, Colorado, Detroit, Fordham, Santa Clara, TCU, Boston College, Tulsa, Oklahoma State, Indiana, Clemson, Missouri.

All-time Top Coaches

Coach	Victories	Coach	Victories
Amos A. Stagg	314	John Heisman	185
Pop Warner	313	Carl Snavely	180
Bear Bryant*	242	Gil Dobie	179
Jess Neely	207	Ben Schwartzwalder	178
Warren Woodson	203	Bob Neyland	173
Woody Hayes*	202	Shug Jordan*	172
Eddie Anderson	201	Wallace Wade	171
Dana X. Bible	198	Ara Parseghian*	170
Dan McGugin	197	Lynn Waldorf	170
Fielding H. Yost	196	Darrell Royal*	169
Howard Jones	194	Red Blaik	166
John Vaught	190		

Coach	Years	Wins	Losses	Ties	Percentage
Knute Rockne	13	105	12	5	.881
Frank Leahy	13	107	13	9	.864
George Woodruff	12	142	25	2	.846
Percy Haughton	13	96	17	6	.832
Bob Neyland	21	173	31	12	.829
Jock Sutherland	20	144	28	14	.812
Bob Devaney	16	136	30	7	.806
Frank Thomas	19	141	33	9	.795
Henry Williams	23	143	34	12	.788
Bo Schembechler	12	98	24	4	.781

* Still active.

Coach	Years	Wins	Losses	Ties	Percentage
Gil Dobie	33	179	45	15	.780
Fred Folsom	19	106	28	6	.779
Frank Kush	17	138	39	1	.778
Fritz Crisler	18	116	32	9	.768
Charley Moran	18	122	33	12	.766
Wallace Wade	24	171	49	10	.765
Dan McGugin	30	197	55	19	.762
Jim Crowley	13	78	21	10	.761
Andy Smith	17	116	32	13	.761
Bear Bryant*	30	242	71	16	.759
Woody Hayes*	29	202	62	8	.757
Darrell Royal*	21	169	53	4	.756
John McKay*	15	119	36	8	.754

* Still active.

Leading Title Coaches

(1900–1974)

Coach	Titles Arbitrary	Titles and Shares	Coach	Titles Arbitrary	Titles and Shares
Howard Jones	4	7	Ara Parseghian*	2	4
Knute Rockne	4	15	Darrell Royal*	2	3
Frank Leahy	3	8	Bob Devaney	2	3
Bud Wilkinson	3	7	Woody Hayes*	1	5
Bernie Bierman	3	7	Wallace Wade	1	5
Pop Warner	3	5	Percy Haughton	1	4
John McKay*	3	5	H. C. Williams	1	4
Bear Bryant*	3	4	Jock Sutherland	1	4
Fritz Crisler	3	4	Amos A. Stagg	1	3
Bob Neyland	2	8	Frank Thomas	1	3
Gil Dobie	2	7	Bill Roper	0	5
Red Blaik	2	6	Joe Paterno*	0	3
Fielding H. Yost	2	4			

*Still active.

Yearly Rankings

(Pre-1900)

(Helms Hall of Fame Champions)

1883
Yale, 8–0–0

1884
Yale, 8–0–1

1885
Princeton, 9–0–0

1886
Yale, 9–0–1

1887
Yale, 9–0–0

1888
Yale, 13–0–0

1889
Princeton, 10–0–0

1890
Harvard, 11–0–0

1891
Yale, 13–0–0

1892
Yale, 13–0–0

1893
Princeton, 11–0–0

1894
Yale, 16–0–0

1895
Penn, 14–0–0

1896
Princeton, 10–0–1

1897
Penn, 15–0–0

1898
Harvard, 11–0–0

1899
Harvard, 10–0–1

1900

YALE, 12–0–0*
Harvard, 10–1–0
Penn, 12–1–0
Minnesota, 8–0–1
Iowa, 7–0–1

1901

MICHIGAN, 11–0–0*
Harvard, 12–0–0
Wisconsin, 9–0–0
Cornell, 11–1–0
Illinois, 9–1–0

1902

MICHIGAN, 11–0–0*
Yale, 11–0–1
Princeton, 8–1–0
Harvard, 11–1–0
Chicago, 11–1–0

1903

PRINCETON, 11–0–0*
Minnesota, 14–0–1
Michigan, 11–0–1
Nebraska, 10–0–0
Notre Dame, 8–0–1

1904

MINNESOTA, 13–0–0
Michigan, 11–0–0
Penn, 12–0–0*
Pitt, 10–0–0
Vanderbilt, 9–0–0

1905

CHICAGO, 9–0–0*
Michigan, 12–1–0
Yale, 10–0–0
Stanford, 8–0–0
Penn, 12–0–1

1906

PRINCETON, 9–0–1*
Yale, 9–0–1
Harvard, 10–1–0
Vanderbilt, 8–1–0
St. Louis 11–0–0

1907

YALE, 9–0–1*
Princeton, 8–2–0
Penn, 10–1–0
Carlisle, 9–1–0
Dartmouth, 8–0–1

1908

PENN, 11–0–1*
Harvard, 9–0–1
Yale, 8–1–1
Chicago, 5–0–1
LSU, 10–0–0

1909

YALE 10–0–0*
Washington, 7–0–0
Harvard, 8–1–0
Notre Dame, 7–0–1
Arkansas, 7–0–0

*Helms Hall of Fame Foundation choice.

1910

WASHINGTON, 7-0-0
Harvard, 8-0-1*
Pitt, 9-0-0
Illinois, 7-0-0
Vanderbilt, 7-0-1

1911

CARLISLE, 11-1-0
Washington, 7-0-0
Princeton, 8-0-2*
Minnesota, 6-0-1
Penn State, 8-0-1

1912

HARVARD, 9-0-0*
Notre Dame, 7-0-0
Penn State, 7-0-0
Wisconsin, 7-0-0
Carlisle, 12-1-1

1913

NOTRE DAME, 7-0-0
Harvard, 9-0-0*
Chicago, 7-0-0
Washington, 7-0-0
Army, 8-1-0

1914

ILLINOIS, 7-0-0
Army, 9-0-0*
Tennessee, 9-0-0
Texas, 8-0-0
Harvard, 7-0-2

1915

PITT, 8-0-0
Cornell, 9-0-0*
Harvard, 8-1-0
Nebraska, 8-0-0
Washington, 7-0-0

1916

ARMY, 9-0-0
Pitt, 8-0-0*
Ohio State, 7-0-0
Georgia Tech, 8-0-1
Minnesota, 6-1-0

1917

GEORGIA TECH, 9-0-0*
Pitt, 9-0-0
Texas A&M, 8-0-0
Ohio State, 8-0-1
Notre Dame, 6-1-1

1918

PITT, 4-1-0*
Texas, 9-0-0
Georgia Tech, 6-1-0
Virginia Tech, 7-0-0
Texas A&M, 6-1-0

1919

NOTRE DAME, 9-0-0
Texas A&M, 10-0-0
Harvard, 9-0-1*
Ohio State, 6-1-0

1920

CALIFORNIA, 9-0-0*
Notre Dame, 9-0-0
Texas, 9-0-0
Ohio State, 7-1-0
Harvard, 8-0-1

1921

IOWA, 7-0-0
California, 9-0-1
Washington & Jefferson, 10-0-1
Cornell, 8-0-0*
Lafayette, 9-0-0

1922

CORNELL, 8-0-0*
California, 9-0-0
Princeton, 8-0-0
Iowa, 7-0-0
Michigan, 6-0-1

1923

ILLINOIS, 8-0-0*
Michigan, 8-0-0
Cornell, 8-0-0
Yale, 8-0-0
SMU, 9-0-0

1924

NOTRE DAME, 10-0-0*
Dartmouth, 7-0-1
Yale, 6-0-2
California, 8-0-2
Alabama, 8-1-0

1925

ALABAMA, 10-0-0*
Dartmouth, 8-0-0
Michigan, 7-1-0
Tulane, 9-0-1
USC, 12-1-0

1926

NAVY, 9-0-1
Alabama, 9-0-1*
Stanford, 10-0-1*
Michigan, 7-1-0
Notre Dame, 9-1-0

1927

TEXAS A&M, 8-0-1
Illinois, 7-0-1*
Georgia, 8-1-0
Yale, 7-1-0
Army, 9-1-0

1928

GEORGIA TECH, 10-0-0*
USC, 9-0-1
Tennessee, 9-0-1
Illinois, 7-1-0
Carnegie Tech, 7-1-0

1929

TULANE, 9-0-0
Notre Dame, 9-0-0*
Purdue, 8-0-0
Tennessee, 9-0-1
TCU, 9-0-1

1930

NOTRE DAME, 10-0-0*
Alabama, 10-0-0
Michigan, 8-0-1
Northwestern, 7-1-0
Tennessee, 9-1-0

1931

TENNESSEE, 9-0-1
USC, 10-1-0*
Tulane, 11-1-0
Alabama, 8-1-0
Pitt, 8-1-0

1932

USC, 10-0-0*
Michigan, 8-0-0
Colgate, 9-0-0
TCU, 10-0-1
Tennessee, 9-0-1

1933

PRINCETON, 9-0-0
Michigan, 7-0-1*
Columbia, 8-1-0
Ohio State, 7-1-0
Pitt, 8-1-0

187

1934

ALABAMA, 10–0–0
Minnesota, 8–0–0*
Pitt, 8–1–0
Navy, 8–1–0
Illinois, 7–1–0

1935

MINNESOTA, 8–0–0*
Princeton, 9–0–0
Stanford, 8–1–0
SMU, 12–1–0
TCU, 12–1–0

Associated Press Rankings

1936

Minnesota, 7–1–0*
LSU, 9–1–1
Pitt, 8–1–1
Alabama, 8–0–1
Washington, 7–2–1
(NORTHWESTERN, 7–1–0†)

1937

PITT, 9–0–1†
California, 10–0–1*
Fordham, 7–0–1
Alabama, 9–1–0
Minnesota, 6–2–0

1938

TCU, 11–0–0*
TENNESSEE, 11–0–0†
Duke, 9–1–0
Oklahoma, 10–1–0
Notre Dame, 8–1–0

1939

TEXAS A&M, 11–0–0*†
Tennessee, 10–1–0
USC, 8–0–2
Cornell, 8–0–0
Tulane, 8–1–1

1940

Minnesota, 8–0–0
STANFORD, 10–0–0*†
Michigan, 7–1–0
Tennessee, 10–1–0
Boston College, 11–0–0

1941

MINNESOTA, 8–0–0*†
Duke, 9–1–0
Notre Dame, 8–0–1
Texas, 8–1–1
Michigan, 6–1–1

* Helms, Citizens' Savings choices
† Book, other choices

1942

Ohio State, 9–1–0
GEORGIA, 11–1–0†
Wisconsin, 8–1–1*
Tulsa, 10–1–0
Georgia Tech, 8–2–0

1943

NOTRE DAME, 9–1–0*†
Iowa PF, 9–1–0
Michigan, 8–1–0
Navy, 8–1–0
Purdue, 9–0–0

1944

ARMY, 9–0–0*†
Ohio State, 9–0–0
Randolph Fd.
Navy, 6–3–1
Bainbridge

1945

ARMY, 9–0–0*†
Alabama, 10–0–0
Navy, 7–1–1
Indiana, 8–0–1
Oklahoma State, 9–0–0

1946

NOTRE DAME, 8–0–1*†
Army, 9–0–1*
Georgia, 11–0–0
UCLA, 10–1–0
Illinois, 8–2–0

1947

Notre Dame, 9–0–0*
MICHIGAN, 10–0–0*†
SMU, 9–0–2
Penn State, 9–0–1
Texas, 10–1–0

1948

MICHIGAN, 9–0–0*†
Notre Dame, 9–0–1
North Carolina, 9–1–1
California, 10–1–0
Oklahoma, 10–1–0

1949

NOTRE DAME, 10–0–0*†
Oklahoma, 11–0–0
California, 10–1–0
Army, 9–0–0
Rice, 10–1–0

Associated Press and United Press International Rankings

AP AND UPI RANKINGS

(AP—Writers, UPI—Coaches)

(1950–1974)

AP

UPI

1950

Oklahoma, 10–1–0*
Army, 8–1–0
Texas, 9–2–0
Tennessee, 11–1–0
California, 9–1–1
KENTUCKY, 11–1–0†

Oklahoma
Texas
Tennessee
California
Army

1951

Tennessee, 10–1–0
Michigan State, 9–0–0*
MARYLAND, 10–0–0†
Illinois, 9–0–1
Georgia Tech, 11–0–1

Tennessee
Michigan State
Illinois
Maryland
Georgia Tech

1952

MICHIGAN STATE, 9–0–0*†
Georgia Tech, 12–0–0
Notre Dame, 7–2–1
Oklahoma, 8–1–1
USC, 10–1–0

Michigan State
Georgia Tech
Notre Dame
Oklahoma (tie)
USC (tie)

AP	UPI

1953

AP	UPI
Maryland, 10–1–0	Maryland
NOTRE DAME, 9–0–1*†	Notre Dame
Michigan State, 9–1–0	Michigan State
Oklahoma, 9–1–1	UCLA
UCLA, 8–2–0	Oklahoma

1954

AP	UPI
Ohio State, 10–0–0*	UCLA
UCLA, 9–0–0*†	Ohio State
Oklahoma, 10–0–0	Oklahoma
Notre Dame, 9–1–0	Notre Dame
Navy, 8–2–0	Navy

1955

AP	UPI
OKLAHOMA, 11–0–0*†	Oklahoma
Michigan State, 9–1–0	Michigan State
Maryland, 10–1–0	Maryland
UCLA, 9–2–0	UCLA
TCU, 9–2–0	Ohio State, 7–2–0

1956

AP	UPI
OKLAHOMA, 10–0–0*†	Oklahoma
Tennessee, 10–1–0	Tennessee
Iowa, 9–1–0	Iowa
Georgia Tech, 10–1–0	Georgia Tech
Texas A&M, 9–0–1	Texas A&M

1957

AP	UPI
AUBURN, 10–0–0*†	Ohio State
Ohio State, 9–1–0	Auburn
Michigan State, 8–1–0	Michigan State
Oklahoma, 10–1–0	Oklahoma
Navy, 9–1–1	Iowa, 7–1–1

1958

AP	UPI
LSU, 11–0–0*†	LSU
Iowa, 8–1–1	Iowa
Army, 8–0–1	Army
Auburn, 9–0–1	Auburn
Oklahoma, 10–1–0	Oklahoma

AP	UPI

1959

AP	UPI
SYRACUSE, 11–0–0*†	Syracuse
Mississippi, 10–1–0	Mississippi
LSU, 9–2–0	LSU
Texas, 9–2–0	Texas
Georgia, 10–1–0	Georgia

1960

AP	UPI
Minnesota, 8–2–0	Minnesota
MISSISSIPPI, 10–0–1†	Iowa
Iowa, 8–1–0	Mississippi
Navy, 10–1–0	Missouri
Missouri, 10–1–0	Washington
Washington, 10–1–0*	

1961

AP	UPI
ALABAMA, 11–0–0*†	Alabama
Ohio State, 8–0–1	Ohio State
Texas, 10–1–0	LSU
LSU, 10–1–0	Texas
Mississippi, 9–2–0	Mississippi

1962

AP	UPI
USC, 11–0–0*†	USC
Wisconsin, 8–2–0	Wisconsin
Mississippi, 10–0–0	Mississippi
Texas, 9–1–1	Texas (tie)
Alabama, 10–1–0	Alabama (tie)

1963

AP	UPI
TEXAS, 11–0–0*†	Texas
Navy, 9–2–0	Navy
Illinois, 8–1–1	Pitt
Pitt, 9–1–0	Illinois
Auburn, 9–2–0	Nebraska, 10–1–0

1964

AP	UPI
Alabama, 10–1–0	Alabama
ARKANSAS, 11–0–0*†	Arkansas
Notre Dame, 9–1–0	Notre Dame
Michigan, 9–1–0	Michigan
Texas, 10–1–0	Texas

AP	UPI

1965

AP	UPI
Alabama, 9–1–1	Michigan State
MICHIGAN STATE, 10–1–0*†	Arkansas
Arkansas, 10–1–0	Nebraska
UCLA, 8–2–1	Alabama
Nebraska, 10–1–0	UCLA

1966

NOTRE DAME, 9–0–1*†	Notre Dame
Michigan State, 9–0–1*	Michigan State
Alabama, 11–0–0	Alabama
Georgia, 10–1–0	Georgia
UCLA, 9–1–0	UCLA

1967

USC, 10–1–0*†	USC
Tennessee, 9–2–0	Tennessee
Oklahoma, 10–1–0	Oklahoma
Indiana, 9–2–0	Notre Dame
Notre Dame, 8–2–0	Wyoming, 10–1–0

1968

OHIO STATE, 10–0–0*†	Ohio State
Penn State, 11–0–0	USC
Texas, 9–1–1	Penn State
USC, 9–1–1	Georgia, 8–1–2
Notre Dame, 7–2–1	Texas

1969

TEXAS, 11–0–0*†	Texas
Penn State, 11–0–0	Penn State
USC, 10–0–1	Arkansas, 9–2–0
Ohio State, 8–1–0	USC
Notre Dame, 8–2–1	Ohio State

1970

NEBRASKA, 11–0–1*†	Texas
Notre Dame, 10–1–0	Ohio State
Texas, 10–1–0	Nebraska
Tennessee, 11–1–0	Tennessee
Ohio State, 9–1–0	Notre Dame

AP	*UPI*

1971

NEBRASKA, 13–0–0*†
Oklahoma, 11–1–0
Colorado, 10–2–0
Alabama, 11–1–0
Penn State, 11–1–0

Nebraska
Alabama
Oklahoma
Michigan, 11–1–0
Auburn. 9–2–0

1972

USC, 12–0–0*†
Oklahoma, 11–1–0
Texas, 10–1–0
Nebraska, 9–2–1
Auburn, 10–1–0

USC
Oklahoma
Ohio State
Alabama, 10–2–0
Texas

1973

NOTRE DAME, 11–0–0*†
Ohio State, 10–0–1
Oklahoma, 10–0–1
Alabama, 11–1–0
Penn State, 12–0–0

Alabama
Oklahoma
Ohio State
Notre Dame
Penn State

1974

OKLAHOMA, 11–0–0*
USC, 10–1–1
Michigan, 10–1–0
Ohio State, 10–2–0
Alabama, 11–1–0

USC
Alabama
Ohio State
Notre Dame, 10–2–0
Michigan

Index

Index

Index

Index

Index